Two-Gether

TWO-GETHER

For people who care enough to share the very best — together

PALMER L. GEDDE

COVER DESIGN BY HAROLD F. SCHMITZ

NORTHWESTERN PUBLISHING HOUSE
Milwaukee, Wisconsin

All rights reserved. Except for brief quotations in critical articles or reviews, no part of this book may be reproduced in any manner without prior written permission from the publisher.

Library of Congress Card 83-61019
Northwestern Publishing House
3624 W. North Ave., Milwaukee, WI 53208-0902
© 1983 by Northwestern Publishing House, All rights reserved
Published 1983
Printed in the United States of America
ISBN 0-8100-0169-1

DEDICATED
to
my children, Terri, Jacki and Peter with the prayer that they will know the full joy of a rich marriage built on the love of our Lord Jesus Christ.

CONTENTS

PREFACE   7

1. UNDERSTANDING OURSELVES   9
2. KNOWING EACH OTHER   21
3. DISCOVERIES ALONG THE WAY   33
4. PROBLEM IDENTIFICATION   43
5. ON COMMUNICATION   57
6. THE "WHY" OF MARRIAGE   71
7. ACCEPTANCE AND FORGIVENESS   81
8. COPING WITH JEALOUSY   91
9. YOUR MARRIAGE CHECKUP   101
10. KEEPING THE MAGIC   113

PREFACE

There is no such thing as a "How To Do It Yourself" marriage book because marriage is never a solo proposition. One person can never build a relationship. What appears to be very obvious does, however, have hidden implications since from the Christian perspective not even two people can build a relationship. It takes three. Unless the marriage is built solidly on the grace of God in Jesus Christ it will at best be an empty and hollow union.

Nevertheless, there are certain skills we can learn and factors we can consider that will aid us in cementing a marriage relationship that is built on a Christian foundation.

It is from this perspective that the following chapters are written. There is no cure-all or answer book that guarantees a good marriage. There are only helps along the way. The effect of these helps will be dependent on the commitment of the marriage partners to openly and honestly discuss them with each other.

This book is essentially a follow-up volume to *One Plus One Equals*. It addresses concerns not covered in the first book. If you do not have or have not read *One Plus One Equals* I would encourage you to get it and study it as a prelude to this volume.

In any event it is my sincere hope that the Holy Spirit will use these pages to enrich your life whether you are preparing for marriage or have experienced the joys and frustrations of marriage for few or many years.

Palmer Gedde

Scripture quotations are from the Revised Standard Version of the Bible, copyright 1946, 1952 C, 1971, and 1972 by the Division of Christian Education of the National Council of Churches, and are used by permission.

UNDERSTANDING OURSELVES 1

Happy is the man who finds wisdom, and the man who gets understanding, for the gain from it is better than gain from silver and its profit better than gold.

Proverbs 3:13,14

10

Understanding Ourselves

"I just don't know what she expects," he said in a troubled and broken voice. "I can't seem to please her regardless of what I say or do. I can't do anything right, I guess. What does she want?"

Similar words have been spoken by both men and women. But regardless of which partner speaks them they are an indication of deep rooted and serious problems within the relationship.

SOURCE

Unfulfilled expectations are usually the source of most difficulties. Expectations inevitably provoke performance measurements and any time we begin to measure the performance level of our spouse there will be disappointments. Why? Because our expectations are often unrealistic. They are usually based on a set of criteria that we have mentally accumulated over the years, criteria that have helped form our behavioral model for ourself and our expectation model for our spouse.

How are such role models formed within us? For the most part, subconsciously, as we observe other people, react to that which we observe, or are influenced by personal experience.

THE IDEAL MATE

Without realizing exactly what is happening we accumulate information throughout our growing years. A daughter will observe her mother as the mother carries out her wife/mother functions and conclude, "When I grow up I want to be just like that." Or, negatively, "When I grow up I am certainly not going to be like that."

The same is true for a son as he observes his father. This information may not be immediately acted on but it is never-

Understanding Ourselves

theless tucked quietly away in the subconscious and finally becomes a part of the individual's understanding of his role model for marriage.

We also develop attitudes towards and form pictures or images of our anticipated mate. A daughter may observe her father and conclude, "I certainly hope that one day I have a husband who treats me that lovingly and considerately." Or, conversely, if the observation prompts a negative response, "I certainly don't want a husband that would do that to me." A boy will have a similar experience as a result of the mental notes he takes while observing his mother's attitudes and actions.

Models are not only formed by observing one's parents. We are also affected by friends, neighbors, relatives, television, books, magazines, movies and the newspaper. All through life, be it ever so subtly, information is gathered and stored. Some of it comes through positive influences and some through negative reactions. But it is there and it is all used to build the mental model of the one we personally picture as the ideal mate. And that information will shape not only our own role model behavior, it will form the basis of our expectations of our spouse.

There is one final input that also shapes our thinking. In addition to projecting real persons into our model making we also project ideals. Every young man dreams of the ideal girl. Every young lady has a mental picture of her knight in shining armor. Fantasizing is also a part of the process.

THE MOMENT

Finally the moment arrives when a young man meets a girl that outwardly at least seems to fit the model he has created. Thereupon he immediately bestows upon her all the qualities of his ideal. Since he is "in love," he fails to

Understanding Ourselves

realize that he doesn't really love the girl as she truly is. In fact he hardly knows her. What he loves is a model, a mental picture of her. As Goethe, the famous German poet and philosopher, said, "My idea of women is not derived from what I have actually seen. It was either inborn in me or else it has grown up inside me in some unfathomable way."

I have heard it said that "Love is blind and marriage is an institution. Therefore marriage is an institution for the blind." In a sense that is true because when love (or whatever you may choose to call it) comes, the person who has fallen in love seldom takes the time necessary to discover the real person with whom he has fallen in love.

PROBLEMS

It usually isn't long after marriage before each partner realizes that at best their ideal is wearing a tainted halo. "Why, he isn't at all like I thought he was." "She was so different before we were married."

What has happened? Each person has started to measure the behavior of the spouse according to the model that was created prior to marriage.

The irony in such measuring is this. Inevitably the problems that surface are not based on issues of right or wrong. They are behavioral expectations and not moral or ethical concerns. The following illustration may help clarify that statement.

A young lady is raised in a home where the father always shook the rugs and vacuumed the carpets on Saturday morning. Her model of an ideal husband therefore included the shaking of the rugs and the vacuuming of the carpets. From her perspective a loving husband would gladly do such chores.

Understanding Ourselves

The young man whom she married had been reared in a home where such duties were women's chores. A husband was not expected to perform such tasks. Therefore his model of a good husband did not include the shaking of rugs or the vacuuming of the carpets.

Neither knew the other's background or feelings on the matter. But when the young man does not shake the rugs or vacuum the carpets, the wife can only assume — on the basis of her model — that he doesn't really love her. Thus, a disappointment, a slight shattering of the ideal as a result of an unfulfilled expectation.

THE PARADOX

The paradox is that the husband felt he was responding appropriately. His role model called for no such action. In fact, to do otherwise would have been a violation of what he believed to be proper.

As a result of her feelings, the lady becomes somewhat distant and reflective. The husband may sense that something is bothering her but from his perspective he cannot imagine what it is.

Who is right and who is wrong in such an instance? The truth is, neither one. Each responded according to what he or she believed to be right. Furthermore, this is not a right or wrong, moral or ethical question. It was simply a problem that had been created by three factors: 1) the role models that had developed over the years, models which were brought as the ideal into the marriage; 2) the fact that they had never discussed their models with each other and therefore neither party had any concept or understanding of the other's expectations; and 3) since there was no awareness of the difference in their models, there had been no negotiation or compromise of these differences.

Understanding Ourselves

THE POINT

The illustration helps to identify the problem. It is also important to note that the problem is neither intentional nor one-sided.

Each partner brings into the relationship two role models. The woman has a model of a good wife and mother, a model that will essentially dictate the manner in which she will attempt to fulfill that role, and a model of the ideal husband, the model by which she will subconsciously measure her spouse.

In like manner the man has two models: a model of a good husband and father, a model that will dictate the manner in which he attempts to fulfill that role, and a model of the ideal wife, the model by which he in turn will subconsciously measure his spouse.

Without any deliberate intention of doing so, the measuring begins. It occurs, however, on more serious matters than shaking the rugs and vacuuming the carpets. It involves life goals, attitudes towards self-discipline, personal hygiene, general abilities and interests, emotional support, habits, sexuality and sexual expectations, raising children, social relationships, spiritual life, recreational interests, money management and a host of other matters. In other words, there is essentially no part of life that is free from some type of role model expectation. And each partner, almost unknowingly, brings all this information into the marriage relationship.

Once again let me affirm that for the most part these are not right or wrong, moral or ethical issues. They simply identify what sort of an end product we are as a result of our background, training, experience, and our learning/thinking process.

A PREMISE

In order for any relationship to survive and grow a couple must first of all recognize and accept the fact that they are both imperfect people, tainted with the mark of sin, who live and function in a fallen creation.

Such a statement could be interpreted as fatalism; that is to say, that all events are inevitable and therefore there is nothing that a person can do to help build a good relationship. That simply is not true. In spite of what we are by nature, we can still learn to act responsibly. Living in and claiming God's grace we can do several things that will help rather than hinder the growth of a relationship and I will speak to those possibilities shortly.

However, it is important that we recognize who and what we are as individuals so that:

1. we do not begin a marriage with totally unrealizable expectations of our mate;

2. we can honestly accept the other as he or she is;

3. we will constantly live in a relationship of understanding and forgiveness;

4. we will take our spouse seriously, respecting his or her right to believe and function as he or she does by accepting each other's model as a legitimate option; and

5. we will talk about our respective models, discover the differences, and negotiate them so that unfair or unrealizable expectations do not hinder growth in the relationship.

TOWARD A SOLUTION

Whether a couple is planning for marriage, has been married for a short time, or a long time, it is appropriate and necessary for them to discuss their models. Far too many marriages are started and continued on the "I didn't know

Understanding Ourselves

that" basis. Obviously a person cannot even begin to fulfill the expectations of his mate if he is not aware of what they are. Furthermore, a person could be doing everything he deems appropriate — and doing it very well according to his model — and completely miss fulfilling the needs and expectations of his spouse.

In some instances there may be expectations that cannot be met regardless of how much it is desired.

My wife is a beautiful 5'2" brunette. I must never expect her to be a 5'10" blonde even though my ideal might have included that characteristic as it was formed in my growing years. For her sake and mine I must hasten to add that I did not have as a characteristic of my ideal a 5'10" blonde. But I trust you see the point.

How can two people discover and resolve their role model differences? I would like to suggest that you try the following exercise. It is an exercise that has been quite helpful to many couples and I use it in both pre-marriage and post-marriage counseling.

Each person is given a sheet of paper with the following captions at the top. On the front side is printed, "My self model." On the flip side, "My mate model."

Each one is asked to carry this paper with them for a two week period. Whenever and wherever an appropriate thought emerges, an idea or statement that fits under one of the captions, they are to write it down. However, they are not to discuss any of the statements that they have written until the end of the two week period.

Assuming that by that time, if they take the exercise seriously, they will each have their models fairly well identified, they are to select a time when they will not be hurried, sit down together, compare their lists, note differences,

Understanding Ourselves

share their respective viewpoints, and begin the process of negotiation and compromise.

This requires a great deal of openness. They need to ask each other, "Why do you feel that way? Is that really important to you and to our marriage?" They also need to be accepting of the other's point of view. And finally they need to ask the question, "Is this a concern that is really important to the success or failure of our marriage?"

The primary purpose of this exercise is to help the couple become aware of themselves, their own thoughts, hopes, and dreams, and of each other. Having experienced the negotiation process they will hopefully recognize the value of this style of communication and continue it throughout their married life.

If there are serious concerns that surface during the exercise the couple will also have the advantage of discussing them with me in one of the following sessions.

CONCLUSION

I sincerely hope you will be encouraged to try this exercise. You cannot fulfill your spouse's expectations if you do not know what they are. Nor can your spouse fulfill yours unless they are known. Certainly it is most beneficial to make these discoveries early in a relationship. Yet it is never too late to learn about ourselves or about the one we have married. If in the process you discover you need help in reconciling some of your role model expectations, get help from your pastor or a professional marriage counselor. Regardless of how long you have been married, or if you are preparing for marriage, an ounce of prevention is always worth a pound of cure.

In the process you could make significant discoveries about each other that might open new doors of understand-

Understanding Ourselves

ing and appreciation. And you can know — if you will only take the time to ask and to hear.

20

KNOWING EACH OTHER 2

By wisdom a house is built, and by understanding it is established; by knowledge the rooms are filled with all precious and pleasant riches.

Proverbs 24:3,4

Knowing Each Other

In the previous chapter the focus was on understanding ourselves. We discovered that it is important to at least attempt understanding because of the different models we bring into the marriage relationship. It was also pointed out that our models are formed over a long period of time and are shaped and influenced by personal experience and other people.

CHANGE

In these pages we will examine the effect that change has on a relationship. To do so we must first recognize that we are constantly changing. I am not the same person now that I was when my wife married me thirty years ago. She is not the exact same person now that she was then. For one thing, we are each thirty years older. During those years we have had many shared experiences that have changed us. We have also had many personal experiences that have affected us. Our behavior patterns and our attitudes have changed.

For example, we are no longer anxious and concerned with the raising of our children since they are now grown and on their own. Consequently we have more freedom to do things and go places. That is one change that affects us as husband and wife but also as individuals.

Every event in life, positive or negative, touches us and changes us. Change is inevitable. But the manner in which two people recognize and accept change in themselves and in each other will ultimately determine how well they really know one another.

IT SOUNDS SO SIMPLE

In the famous Broadway musical, "The King and I," there is a song titled "Getting to know you." The lyrics read as

Knowing Each Other

follows. Perhaps you remember them.
Getting to know you,
getting to know all about you.
Getting to like you,
getting to hope you like me.
Getting to know you,
putting it my way, but nicely,
you are precisely my cup of tea.
Getting to know you,
getting to feel free and easy.
When I am with you,
getting to know what to say.
Haven't you noticed, suddenly I'm bright and breezy?
Because of all the beautiful and new
things I'm learning about you,
day by day.

It all sounds so casual, so positive, so matter of fact. It is suggested by these words that all two people have to do to get to know each other is to be together. There is no doubt about it, that certainly helps. But just being together is no guarantee that things will turn out just fine or that you will truly get to know the other person.

The truth is, trying to get to know another person intimately may be one of the most frustrating, but also exciting, ventures you ever undertake. Indeed, after a life-time of sharing and living together you may discover there is still much that you do not know about your spouse.

A BIG LITTLE WORD

It is interesting to note that in both the Old and New Testaments the word that is used to describe an intimate sexual relationship is the word "know." In Genesis 4:1 we read, "Now Adam *knew* Eve his wife, and she conceived

Knowing Each Other

and bore Cain. . . ." In Matthew 1:24-25 we read, "When Joseph woke from sleep, he did as the angel of the Lord commanded him; he took his wife, but *knew* her not until she had borne a son; and he called his name Jesus."

From the Biblical perspective the word "know" suggests a very personal knowledge. It literally means to know another in the innermost, to be aware of that which runs deep within the spirit of another, to know that which makes an individual what he or she is.

IMPOSSIBLE

Does that heading frighten or startle you? It is not intended to. But it does identify a truth that we must accept and with which we must learn to deal.

Even though the desire to know another intimately runs strong within us, the ability to know another fully is literally impossible. There are essentially three reasons for that.

First, as has already been stated, we are constantly changing. Have you ever noticed that just about the time you think you have someone all figured out he throws you a curve ball and you end up saying to yourself, "That's a surprise. I certainly never expected that out of him."

Life is not lived in a vacuum. Life is not static or dormant. It is not free from the effects and influences of people and places. Day by day our experiences mold us. Some have a positive influence; others, a negative influence. But whatever the circumstance, the events of the day leave their mark on us. Not a one among us is exactly the same as we were yesterday. Therefore, in our personal relationships we are involved in a process, the process of becoming better acquainted in many areas, newly acquainted in some, but never completely acquainted in all. As long as there is change there will always be something to learn.

Knowing Each Other

Secondly, we will only know others to the degree they allow themselves to be known to us. You may have a great deal of information about another person and still not know him. You might, for example, know how old, how tall, how heavy he is. You might know where he was born, his vocation, his hobbies, his likes and dislikes, the size of his family, his preference in clothes, his salary, and a host of other facts.

But what are his attitudes, weaknesses, his joys and sorrows? For what does he yearn deep in his spirit? Where does he find strength and comfort? What are his hopes and dreams for both the present and future? These things you will never know unless he chooses to share them with you.

So it is even in the intimate relationship of marriage. You will ultimately know your spouse only as he allows himself to be known to you.

Thirdly, every individual has private, personal corners in his life that are his alone. There are special moments that each of us have experienced, or may experience, that have meaning only for us. I am not talking about skeletons in the closet. I am here referring to gifts given us, in some instances spiritual gifts — mountaintop moments from the hand of a loving Father. I am also talking about those needed strokes that speak the word of "well done" or "thank you."

Such moments may remain hidden within us simply because they are ours and really have no meaning to anyone else. But we need to recognize that they do exist in our own life and in the life of our spouse. Honor that hiddenness, that privateness, in your spouse. It is not a threat to a relationship. It is simply a recognition of one's individuality.

RATHER REJOICE

How do we deal with the fact, then, that we will never really get to know the one with whom we nonetheless share the greatest intimacies? Should we throw in the towel and say, "Why try"?

Not at all. Discovery can be exciting since it is also an indication of trust. For example: the more completely my wife allows herself to be known by me, the greater the evidence of her trust in me.

We never open ourselves up to someone we do not trust. No one wants to get hurt or walked on. Every individual experiences enough hurt without deliberately making himself vulnerable needlessly.

Essentially we have two choices in this matter of knowing each other. We can either be frustrated, sometimes to the point of despair, because of the realization we will never really know our spouse due to the change factors. Or we can rejoice in each new discovery we do make, each new understanding that is shared, each insight that is given, accepting them as signs of ever increasing love and trust.

MAKING THE ADJUSTMENTS

Since you are both changing persons, negotiation is not only necessary as an occasional option, it is essential on a continuing basis. The American College Dictionary defines "negotiate" as follows: "to arrange for or bring about by discussion and settlement of terms; to clear or pass an obstacle."

The circumstances and conditions of your life together will change. So will your attitudes and expectations. Unless you are able to really negotiate these changes by talking about them, as you sense change in yourself, in your spouse, or in your situation, and by coming to some mutually satisfying decision you will only find yourselves drifting apart rather than growing more closely together.

Making such adjustments and negotiating your differences is essentially a sign of your love. After all, a solid marriage relationship can never be built if two people are determined to go their own direction and fight for their own identity.

The biblical word for love, *agape*, means, "the willingness to give oneself totally in behalf of the other without expectation or measurement." Such love is more than willing to make adjustments and negotiate. It is constantly seeking the other's well-being and welfare.

So if you truly love one another, you will be anxious to share, discuss and respond. As you discover more clearly each other's faults and virtues, you will also learn how to get on best with each other whatever the circumstances of life.

WHAT WE CAN KNOW THAT WILL HELP

We live in an age that emphasizes the equality of men and women. Much of that is long overdue. Equality, however, does not mean "alike." There are significant differences between the two. In Genesis we are reminded that even though the woman was a human being like the man — "This at last is bone of my bones and flesh of my flesh" (Genesis 2:23) — she was still different.

There was, and is, a sexual difference and a physical difference between men and women. But there are many good books available to you that discuss those attributes. Therefore I will only mention them in the hope that you will take them seriously, study them in order to better understand each other, and accept the differences as a part of the uniqueness that draws you together.

Knowing Each Other

Perhaps the most significant difference is the psychological or personality difference. It can certainly be said that men and women have a difficult time understanding each other. This is primarily due to the fact that each tends to judge the other according to his own sex.

How often have you heard a man say, "I'll never understand a woman." He has a point, because he never really will. But what he is really complaining about is that a woman doesn't function or act exactly like a man.

Similarly a woman may say, "That's just like a man for you." I suspect that such a statement is not intended to be complimentary either. She really means, "How unfortunate that you men are not like us women."

What is the basis for this difference? Masculinity and femininity. Let me be quick to add that I do not believe these are "bad" words. They are not chauvinistic. They are descriptive and functional terms.

DEFINITION

When we use the term "masculinity" we think of strength. Physically a man is normally stronger than a woman and is therefore less likely to be physically overcome. From that perspective the word "masculine" suggests stability, security and strength.

The word "feminine" or "femininity" also suggests strength, but strength of a different kind. Feminine strength suggests warmth, tenderness and sensitivity.

One is not better or superior to the other. Indeed they complement each other and form a oneness that the Bible describes as "one flesh" (Genesis 2:24). Nevertheless, each will exert itself in very specific ways.

EXAMPLE

Take for example the manner in which these two roles express themselves in sexual intercourse. Indeed the man must prove his masculinity or there will be no intercourse. This also suggests that a woman will be fulfilled in this most intimate relationship only to the degree that a husband is able to demonstrate his masculinity. The woman's role, even though she may be the aggressor in initiating the activity, is nevertheless passive in so far as she must accept and receive.

Let me state again that this is not an issue of one person being better than another, of inferiority or superiority. It is merely the statement of a fact that in the sexual relationship the male must exert his masculinity, his strength role.

There is also a difference in the masculine and feminine outlook on things. A man tends to look at things objectively while a woman views things more subjectively. A man will tend to take something apart in order to see what makes it tick. He moves through an issue in a logical manner inevitably arriving at the conclusion that because two and two equal four there is a logical reason behind actions and responses.

A woman will view things as a whole. She tends to see things as they are, black or white, without analyzing or scrutinizing. For her two and two may not equal four or they may be more than four. It all depends on the circumstances. Instinct may be utilized in decision making rather than logic.

CONCLUSION

This is not by any means intended to be an exhaustive study of all the differences. But it is intended to point out that there certainly are some. They are there because of the way we have been fashioned by the hand of a loving God. Be aware of the differences. Accept them. Take the time to learn about each other for learning will assist in understanding.

Perhaps this last section of the chapter could be summarized as follows. Normally each of us has two eyes. If you lose the sight in one eye, be it by accident or simply by covering it, you will notice that things appear flat. There is no dimension or perspective. It takes both eyes working together to see things as they really are.

So it is in the husband/wife relationship. The differences complement and thereby create a whole, a whole that is the unique combination of all that two individuals bring into the relationship.

In spite of the fact that there may be a great deal you will never know about your spouse, there is still the possibility for great excitement and joy as a result of the discoveries you do make. Just don't stop discovering or thanking God for the special gift that is yours in your spouse.

32

DISCOVERIES ALONG THE WAY 3

Set me as a seal upon your heart, as a seal upon your arm; for love is strong as death, jealousy is cruel as the grave. Its flashes are flashes of fire, a most vehement flame. Many waters cannot quench love, neither can floods drown it.

Song of Solomon 8:6,7

34

Discoveries Along The Way

As a little boy I looked forward with great anticipation to those occasions when my father would allow me to drive the family automobile. It was a wonderful feeling to take the wheel of that 1936 Ford. There was an overwhelming sense of power as that flathead V8 moved gingerly down the road. I remember that Dad used to sit slightly towards the middle of the front seat — just in case: just in case I got into a situation that I could not handle. From that vantage point he knew that he could quickly grab the steering wheel, step on the brake, or shut off the ignition if need be. I really didn't mind his being there. It gave me a sense of security and confidence.

Like all boys, I could hardly wait for the day to come when I was old enough to get my driver's license. My dreams were filled with the expectations of taking the car all by myself.

It wasn't long, however, before I learned what all young drivers must learn. Driving isn't all milk and honey. Bad weather can make driving anything but fun. And there are all those other careless drivers coming down the road right at you. I also discovered that having a tire blow out at highway speed will make a person sit up and take notice.

When I had friends along, there was an awesome sense of responsibility for their well-being. Even though the automobile was not new, I was well aware of the fact that my father wanted no additional marks or scratches on it.

The point is: what I once thought to be all joy and delight turned out to be much more than that. It also meant coping with the unexpected, assuming responsibility, having to be on the alert at all times and being extremely careful. It wasn't so simple after all.

DISCOVERY

I had made a very important discovery. The question is:

how was I going to handle such a discovery? Essentially I had two alternatives. One alternative was to decide that I didn't need all that hassle and therefore I wouldn't drive any more. The other alternative was to accept the fact that such conditions went with driving and that if I expected to experience the joy of travel I would also have to accept the responsibilities.

In addition to that I also had to prepare myself for handling new experiences, new situations that I had not yet encountered. There would be many more discoveries down the road.

MARRIAGE

Marriage in the fullest sense is a lifelong adventure in which two people commit themselves to discovery. It is an on-going process which like driving usually begins with great expectation and anticipation. When a couple actually starts down the marriage road they inevitably discover that things are not quite like they expected. More times than I care to remember a disenchanted spouse has said, "If I had only known."

I suspect that in many premarriage relationships the two people are more in love with the idea of marriage than they are with each other. How easy it is for one's vision to be clouded when he is overwhelmed with the feeling of love. Looking at the relationship as a whole through objective lenses is not that easy even though, as pointed out in the first two chapters of this book, it is essential.

What if two people seriously try to evaluate themselves, their relationship, and their expectations? Can such a process eliminate all the questions? Probably not. One not so young lad (he is twenty-seven) who is presently involved with his spouse in premarital counseling stated it this way, "I

Discoveries Along The Way

keep wondering when the bubble is going to break. We seem to fit together too good." I don't like to see a couple approach marriage with the idea that "the bubble is going to break," but he had recognized a significant truth. Regardless of the preparation for marriage there still are going to be discoveries along the way, discoveries that will inevitably affect the relationship and raise questions, and issues, that the couple must work through together.

WHEN THE BUBBLE BREAKS

The intensity of her concern was indicated by the tone of her voice. "Pastor, can John and I come in to talk with you right now?" Even though I was practically out the door on my way to another commitment it was very clear that this request had to be given priority.

A short time later they were in my office. For several minutes they both sat quietly. Finally the silence was broken as she began to share her concerns. The story was a familiar one filled with broken promises, unmet needs, and unrealized expectations. In an almost pleading and apologetic voice he finally commented, "What does she expect? After all, I am only human."

Indeed, after marriage, the discovery of our spouse's humanness can be quite a surprise. Prior to marriage a person is likely to be on his best behavior since the marriage is still at stake. No one wants to botch up what he thinks is going to be the best thing that ever happened to him. After marriage there is the tendency to relax, to pay less attention to details, to be less considerate of the other's needs and feelings, to be less observant. Each will take the other more for granted. Faults that were apparent become more obvious and are intensified through day by day contact and living. Little things that were overlooked become genuine annoyances and at times are viewed as deliberate carelessness. This might include everything from squeezing the toothpaste tube on the wrong end to forgetting a birthday or an anniversary.

When a marriage finally gets to the place where tension is evident, the two people, like the boy learning to drive, have two choices. One option is the choice that far too many people are following today: divorce. It is the decision to avoid the problems and ignore the hassle, by simply removing one's self from that which causes the struggle.

The second option calls for serious commitment but it is the only pathway that will also lead to fulfillment. Here the couple recognizes and admits that such discoveries are a normal and natural part of living together. Both will accept their own humanness and the failings and faults of the other. Certainly each person will work toward changing those things in his life that irritate and hurt his spouse, if they can be changed. There will be openness in sharing feelings, discussion on how to correct a difficulty, and mutuality in working together to change both cause and effect. Most important, the relationship will be based on the will of God, who intends marriage to be a lifelong union. Such a relationship calls for understanding and commitment. But I will say more about these subjects later.

POSITIVE OR NEGATIVE

As a starting point towards a possible and positive solution for handling discoveries along the way, let me offer the following counsel. There is always the danger that a counselor can be over simplistic in his approach or in his recommendation of a method to be tried. This is not intended to be such a suggestion even though at first glance it might appear to be so. I am well aware of the fact that some issues that

Discoveries Along The Way

surface as a result of discovery have deep rooted causes and serious implications and are therefore not easily resolved.

Nevertheless, I am firmly convinced that many problems can be laid to rest if people will approach them from a positive rather than negative attitude. For lack of a better example let me share a personal illustration.

TERRIBLE FEET

Unfortunately there are people in this world who are plagued with an annoying, and at times embarrassig, problem: smelly feet. I happen to be one such person. Doctors have given me prescriptions and friends have suggested remedies — all to no avail. I can wash them ten times a day, powder them, deodorize them, change socks and shoes, air them, pamper them . . . it makes no difference. They perspire and give off a less than pleasant odor.

Prior to our marriage I managed to keep that bit of information well hidden from my wife. Yet there was always the anticipation of her finding out how bad they were. What would she think? How would she react? What would she say?

It wasn't long after we were married that the truth surfaced. She could have reacted negatively. "If I had only known how terrible his feet really were, I would never have gotten into this situation. It's repulsive. I have to air out the house every time he takes off his shoes. I just don't know how much of that I can take."

She chose to respond positively. "There's one thing for sure," she would say. "As long as his feet smell I know he's still alive. Furthermore, I always know where he is."

Discoveries Along The Way

IMPLICATIONS

Attitudes do make a difference. In a loving fashion she was able to turn what was obviously a negative into a positive. There are many such instances when "putting the most charitable construction on all that is said and done," as Luther encourages us to do in his explanation to the Eighth Commandment, will change a frown to a smile, a disappointment to a delight, or a frustration to a victory.

There are other implications, too. Early in a relationship a person might not consider how he will react later on to that which is very appealing at the time. When he spent his money freely on you before marriage, you thought, "How nice." After marriage you may think "How careless can someone be." You used to boast to your friends about how easygoing he was. Now his easygoing nature has all the appearance of laziness. He used to delight in your quiet manner. Now it is seen as indifference or moodiness.

We need to understand that there are differences in temperament between men and women. You ought not be surprised to discover after marriage that your temperaments differ. No two people think exactly alike, work the same way, handle problems identically, or respond the same — even in similar situations. Discovering your differences should supplement and strengthen your relationship, not tear it down. And it can, if you deal with the differences in a positive and supportive manner.

NEW TERRITORY

Larry and Nordis Christenson in their book, *The Christian Couple*, write: "Marriage is like the conquest and settling of a new land. When you cross from single to married life it is like a pioneer crossing the Mississippi River in 1840 — a new unexplored territory stretches out before you. No

Discoveries Along The Way

matter how many people have settled down in marriage before, it is still a new and unsettled land for each couple that enters into it."

I like that. Discovering the wholeness of another person in the intimacies of marriage can be a great adventure if, in patience, you take the time to try and understand each other, recognizing that your relationship is unique because you as individuals are unique. Never before in the history of mankind has there been a combination of backgrounds, attitudes, experiences, abilities and personalities like yours. There never will be again. Therefore you are special persons, a special couple.

Let each other's specialness be received positively as you make discoveries along the way. Accepting your spouse as he or she is because God so graciously accepts you as you are, will turn even the unexpected into glad surprises.

42

PROBLEM IDENTIFICATION 4

Love is patient and kind; love is not jealous or boastful; it is not arrogant or rude. Love does not insist on its own way; it is not irritable or resentful; it does not rejoice at wrong, but rejoices in the right. Love bears all things, believes all things, hopes all things, endures all things.

1 Corinthians 13:4-7

Problem Identification

Perhaps it was the cloudy, dismal day. It seems difficulties are magnified when the weather is bad. Whatever the reason, my phone had been ringing steadily from the moment I arrived at the office. The intercom buzzer noisily announced another call.

"Yes?" I inquired. "It's a Mrs. Williams on line one" my secretary responded. Her request was straightforward and urgent. "May I come in to see you right away?"

A few minutes later Mrs. Williams was seated in my office. For several moments she just sat there trying to gain her composure. Tears moved slowly down her cheeks. Every so often she gathered them gently into the white tissue that was clutched in her hand. I waited and watched.

Finally the first halting words were spoken. "Pastor, John and I have a serious problem." "What is it?" I asked. "I don't know," she replied. "I really don't know. I just know we have a problem. Will you help us?"

A PROBLEM?

It was not the first time I had heard such a statement. I suspect it will not be the last. The clue that helped explain her particular situation was in the response, "I don't know." And she didn't. All she knew was that her relationship with her husband had reached a breaking point. Unless something changed and changed quickly she was convinced the marriage would not survive.

She and John had been married for nearly six years. Their relationship, from an observer's point of view, had been no worse or better than many others. John tended to keep his feelings to himself. But so do a lot of people. He was not a man who wore his feelings on his shirt sleeves. Neither did she for that matter.

Problem Identification

They were both essentially rational people. What had happened? How did their relationship get to this point? What was the problem?

The reason she could not identify a specific problem was because there wasn't *a problem*. There were several problems. During their six years of marriage a number of small difficulties had gone unresolved. Since each seemed to be rather insignificant at the time it was mentally dismissed with the belief that it would eventually correct itself or disappear.

The difficulty was, and is, unresolved problems do not go away. Each is stored in a person's memory bank of disappointments and hurts. Sooner or later the storehouse gets full. The proverbial straw that breaks the camel's back may be another of those seemingly inconsequential moments. Added to those that have previously gone unresolved the load finally gets too heavy to carry. Perhaps it results in a verbal explosion. Maybe it manifests itself in a quiet turning away from one's spouse. However it finally occurs, the relationship is nevertheless broken.

A DIAGRAM TO AID IN UNDERSTANDING

Our tendency is to think that a broken relationship comes as a result of "A PROBLEM." A person has difficulty in identifying that problem.

"A PROBLEM" is invariably several unresolved problems that have been allowed to accumulate over a period of time.

PURPOSE

Before proceeding further I believe it is important to state the specific purpose of this chapter. These pages are not intended to provide easy answers or quick solutions to problems. Indeed, as any counselor will readily acknowledge, there are no easy solutions for mending broken relationships.

These pages are rather intended to help you identify potential, or existing, problem areas and the conditions that tend to breed problems if these conditions are left unattended. That is to say, I will not be suggesting problem solving mechanisms. It is rather my intention to suggest several *problem identification* mechanisms. If you can identify the little monsters when they first rear their ugly heads and get rid of them early you will very likely be able to avoid the giant monster that is most elusive and extremely difficult to manage and identify.

POTENTIAL PROBLEM AREAS

In previous chapters we discussed role models and expectations, the limitations and possibilities that are yours in knowing each other, and how to handle discoveries along the way. All are potential problem areas. In this section we will attempt to identify a few of the more elusive problem areas which, if left unresolved or unattended, can be equally as serious and problematic.

For identification purposes I have divided them into two categories: influences from within, and influences from without.

INFLUENCES FROM WITHIN

1. *Faith Issues.* Even though the Christian faith is personal, it is never private. Throughout the New Testament

Problem Identification

the writers speak of the corporate nature of faith. A believer is never a believer in isolation. He is a part of a larger body (1 Corinthians 12:12,13). It is within the fellowship that faith is nurtured and grows. Or so it should be. Faith never remains stationary. It will grow or it will die but it does not remain the same. The fellowship of believers, living their life together around Word and Sacrament, serves as the nurturing community for growth. That is the reason it is so important to be an active, faithful part of a Christian congregation.

Jesus said, "Where two or three are gathered in my name, I am in the midst of them" (Matthew 18:20). "Two" can mean husband and wife. Therefore even in the intimate relationship of marriage there is corporate identity. It should be a spiritually nurturing community.

Far too often faith concerns are placed on the "we will take care of that later" list. In some instances one partner may have the desire to build the marriage on Christ and in the church while the other either sees no need or wants any part of it. If this is the case the partner who wants to grow spiritually will be forced to struggle alone. What is rightly intended to be a uniting factor can turn into a divisive factor if the partners become ever more distant in their faith-life.

Since marriage is a holy relationship, instituted by God, it behooves a couple to build their life together on the One who can and will sanctify it with his presence. Such a lifestyle requires sharing, caring, decision and learning. Unwillingness on the part of either partner will create a spiritual gap in the relationship. If two people do not share on the spiritual level of their marriage, they settle for much less than God intends and much less than could be experienced.

If you as a couple are not united on matters of faith, you can be certain that sooner or later a problem will arise that will force you to make a decision between the one you love and the call to faithfulness that our Lord Jesus requires. Truly an ounce of prevention is worth a pound of cure. Build your life together from the beginning of your marriage on Jesus Christ and those concerns that could turn into barriers will turn to blessings.

2. *The Romance Fallacy.* A deep, inner, unrealistic longing for romantic highs can actually be destructive to marriage. People can have unrealizable expectations. Marriage is not always romance or romantic. That is not to say that there shouldn't be romance in marriage. Of course there should be. But to live with the illusion that it will or must always be filled with romantic delight is to deny the reality of the relationship. No one, however amorous he may be, can constantly beguile his partner. Because we are sinful by nature and our relationship will be affected by our sinfulness and selfishness, marriage will not always be a rose garden. For that matter we would do well to remember that even the roses have thorns. And in spite of their outward beauty and appeal they are nevertheless subject to disease and death. It is tragic how movies, television and advertising constantly tantalize the American public with completely unrealistic images of relationships based solely on physical attraction and romance.

The constant need for romance is little more than narcissism turned inside out. Any marriage that is based on purely selfish motives is bound to falter. It is much better to learn to love maturely, with respect and tenderness, supporting and building up each other. Let your romance be self-giving rather than self-seeking.

3. *Lack of Self-Esteem.* We have all heard the cliche, "Pride goes before the fall." Nevertheless, the opposite of pride can be just as destructive. If you have no feeling of

Problem Identification

self-worth you will be little good to yourself or to your partner. If you accept and like yourself for what you are you will be secure enough to handle any difficulty that occurs.

We live in a difficult age. We are constantly bombarded with models of how we should look, act, feel and be. It is extremely easy to feel that we must measure up to these imposed standards. If in our own judgment we do not, we feel like second-class persons.

We all need to hear, and remember, that it is just fine to be who and what we are as individuals. After all, in God's eyes we are each special. He made only one like you, only one like me. God obviously felt that he had done a good enough job to warrant throwing away the mold. Moreover, we know from the Bible how he sent his Son to redeem us and the Holy Spirit to sanctify us. If we have that kind of worth in his eyes, we can certainly have worth in our own eyes.

4. *Our Own Flesh.* Martin Luther describes man's greatest enemies as "sin, the devil, and our own flesh." The needs and desires of the flesh can also create problems in marriage. Call them what you may: power, possessions, prestige, authority, position, money, greed, pride, lust . . . if they go unchecked and become the motivating force that controls and drives us, there will be difficulties in a relationship. They may well lead to disaster.

We should remember that while it takes two to build a relationship, it only takes one to break it. The flesh, which is that which we are by nature, can cause us so completely to focus our attention and energy on self, our own goals, needs, and ambitions, that our spouse is literally left out of our life.

INFLUENCES FROM WITHOUT

1. *Money Concerns.* Disagreements concerning money

Problem Identification

usually conceal deeper problems that have to do with control, competition and self-esteem. The manner in which a person deals with or handles money tells a great deal about what a person expects from a relationship.

Being tight with money can reflect selfishness. Being careless with money can suggest immaturity. Since money does provide most of our basic life needs, we are concerned about the manner in which it flows in and out of our lives.

The loss of employment can amplify concern. Overspending, misuse of credit cards, or overextending on larger credit responsibilities can create enormous tension in marriage. Certain conditions over which we have no control, such as illness or inflation, can also arise to trouble us. We ought to always, however, give careful attention to our individual attitude concerning money so that we do not allow those matters *over which we do have control* to get out of hand.

Money and the ability to earn it are gifts from God. Treat the entire matter of money from the perspective of being a responsible steward of a good gift that is intended to enhance life, not thwart it.

2. The Arrival of Children. The arrival of a child is truly one of the greatest blessings a husband and wife will ever experience. At the same time it will require one of the greatest adjustments two people will ever face. A new baby causes a change in lifestyle, spending habits and roles. All three of these affect a relationship.

Nevertheless, children provide a totally unique opportunity for growth and wonderful new experiences as long as the parents do not become so overwhelmed with parenting that they forget their primary responsibility to each other and their marriage.

3. *The Devil.* The Apostle Peter writes, "Be sober, be watchful. Your adversary the devil prowls around like a roaring lion, seeking someone to devour" (1 Peter 5:8).

Remember well that Satan's power may not be so much felt in his direct confrontation with you as in his attempt to influence and control you. If he can succeed in getting you to be careless, indifferent or self-centered in your marriage, there is no need for direct action or confrontation. He much prefers to accomplish his divisive purposes through the quiet manipulation of your thoughts and values.

4. *The World Around Us.* Who of us is not confronted with the challenge to succeed, at least by the world's standards of success? The desire for position, prestige, power, money, fame, making our personal mark and security haunts us all. Let us be very careful lest we be overwhelmed by that which fades and has no eternal value. The world's measurements and standards and God's are not the same. Therefore we would do well to examine our goals regularly. "Therefore I tell you, do not be anxious about your life, what you shall eat or what you shall drink, nor about your body, what you shall put on. Is not life more than food, and the body more than clothes? . . . Seek first his kingdom and his righteousness, and all these things will be yours as well" (Matthew 6:25,33).

CONDITIONS THAT BREED PROBLEMS

This paragraph will be very brief. Listed below are six items that can generate problems if they are not worked through by a couple. I share them with you primarily for the purpose of identification. If any of these conditions exist in your relationship you would do well to discuss them and if need be seek the help of a professional counselor to resolve them.

Problem Identification

1. Failure to, or inability to, negotiate differences. You have heard the statement: "There is your way, my way, and the right way." Very often that is true. The *right way* is the way that allows two people to reach a decision or conclusion that is acceptable to both.
2. Expecting one's spouse to conform, especially in the way he or she thinks.
3. Lack of spiritual unity and common direction.
4. Absence of approval and appreciation of and for each other.
5. Moving in separate directions: i.e., interests, hobbies, friends, life style, personal goals, etc.
6. Placing undue importance on things, not enough on each other.

SIGNS THAT INDICATE PROBLEMS

1. Game playing (not being honest with each other).
2. Power struggle (the attempt to control the relationship).
3. Money control.
4. "I don't want to talk about it."
5. Confrontation rather than compassion (pointing the finger at the other person).
6. Affection shown only in order to have sexual needs fulfilled.
7. Mistrust, often expressed by questioning. "How much did you pay for that dress? I just can't trust you with money." "Why can't you ever remember what I told you?" "Can't you get anything right?"
8. Complaining or nagging.

Problem Identification

QUESTIONS

Listed below are five important questions that you can ask about your marriage relationship. (I am certain there are more you can add to the list.) A "Yes" response will indicate a problem area.

1. Are there angry words spoken more often than kind words?
2. Are there specifically touchy subjects that trigger quick reactions?
3. Are earlier kindnesses and courtesies disappearing from the relationship?
4. Is there a tendency to *hassle* that goes beyond kidding?
5. Has either of you ever physically struck the other?

CONCLUSION

There is a danger associated with problem indentification. It could lead to the mistaken notion that if there is a difficulty in the marriage it is heading toward inevitable disaster. Not at all. Consider the following.

1. Silver and gold are refined by the hottest of fires. A relationship can actually grow stronger through struggling with a difficulty, *if* the couple does not let it overwhelm them.
2. Recognizing a problem is half the solution to it. If a relationship isn't right, both partners sense it. The loving course of action is to search together to try and uncover the problem. Ignoring a difficulty will never make it disappear. By working through the smaller difficulties individually as they occur they will not accumulate into a larger unidentifiable problem.

Problem Identification

3. If in the process you discover that you are unable to resolve a problem through your own efforts, seek professional assistance.

ON COMMUNICATION 5

If we live by the Spirit, let us also walk by the Spirit. Let us have no self-conceit, no provoking of one another, no envy of one another.

Galatians 5:25,26

58

On Communication

Much has been written about the importance of, need for, and lack of communication in marriage. Why, then, the need for still another chapter on what is apparently an old subject? Because I believe it is important to state a premise that is often ignored or at least not always acknowledged. It may surprise you that I should make such a statement but if you think it through carefully you will probably find yourself agreeing with it. The premise is:

There is no such thing as a lack of communication in any marriage.

IS THAT SO?

When the word *communicate* is used to describe a condition that exists or does not exist in a marriage relationship it is invariably used in reference to oral communication; that is, talking or speaking. Communication, however, is much more than that and it takes place through an assortment of techniques. A person will use whatever method works, or seems necessary, to make his feelings known.

On that basis let me repeat the premise. *There is no such thing as a lack of communication in any marriage.* There is negative communication and positive communication but there is never an absence of it. If a person is sensitive to this truth he will discover that even silence can speak very loudly.

DEFINITION

It seems appropriate to start with a definition of the word, communication. *The American College Dictionary* defines it as follows: 1) act or fact of communicating; transmission. 2) the imparting or interchange of thoughts, opinions, or information by speech, writing, or signs. 3) that which is communicated or imparted.

On Communication

Did you notice that in addition to speech, writing and *signs* were also listed. That's very important to know since in a marriage relationship *signs* are often used more frequently than any other technique. It's also necessary to recognize the fact that *signs* can be verbal as well as non-verbal.

ILLUSTRATION

A man told me that he used to become terribly upset with his wife's apparent inability to keep the house in order. After living in what he categorized as an "awful mess" for a couple of weeks he would start with the verbal jabs. This went on for several years. The verbal jab was not oral communication in the sense of sharing or talking. It was a *sign*. It was a technique that he used in order to "get things straightened out."

About a year ago he realized what he was doing. First of all, he recognized that he had never offered to help her with the problem. He had assumed that she had both the ability and the time to do it but that she was incapable of managing her time well. When he finally talked with her about his feelings he made an interesting discovery. The demands placed on her by the children were far greater than he had realized. In fact, because of their particular circumstances, his expectations were quite unrealistic.

But secondly, and undoubtedly most important, he discovered that he had hurt her very deeply by his verbal jabbing. *He* had hurt *her*. The *sign* he had used got the house straightened but in the process he had unintentionally created a much more serious problem.

A BIBLICAL ADMONITION

In Colossians 3:12-19 St. Paul gives some extremely valu-

On Communication

able counsel concerning what could be called a biblical communications attitude. As you read these words think about what they suggest regarding the manner in which two people should try to communicate with each other.

"Put on then, as God's chosen ones, holy and beloved, compassion, kindness, lowliness, meekness, and patience, forbearing one another, and if one has a complaint against another, forgiving each other; as the Lord has forgiven you, so you also must forgive. And above all these put on love, which binds everything together in perfect harmony. And let the peace of Christ rule in your hearts, to which indeed you were called in the one body. And be thankful. Let the word of Christ dwell in you richly, as you teach and admonish one another in all wisdom, and as you sing psalms and hymns and spiritual songs with thankfulness in your hearts to God. And whatever you do, in word or deed, do everything in the name of the Lord Jesus, giving thanks to God the Father through him. Wives, be subject to your husbands as is fitting in the Lord. Husbands, love your wives and do not be harsh with them."

Here we see the beautiful way in which Christians are to communicate with each other — in love, kindness, forgiveness, patience and so on. Everything is to be done with Christ the Savior in our hearts. He loved us and gave himself for us. So we are to love one another and give of ourselves. He forgives us our sins. So we are to learn to forgive each other. He has established peace between God and us. So we should live in peace with each other.

We grow in the Christian life as we remain close to God's Word, the Holy Bible. Christian couples will not only want to attend church each week, but also regularly read the Bible together in home devotions.

In the paragraphs that follow, with this scriptural admoni-

On Communication

tion as background, we will consider eight factors that significantly influence communication patterns in a husband-wife relationship. They are shared with the hope that they will stimulate you to think carefully about your own understanding of communication, encourage you in those areas where you are experiencing success, and assist you where you need help and guidance.

1. CONDITIONS THAT LEND THEMSELVES TO COMMUNICATION

A. Reflect on those occasions or situations when it was easy for you to share your true feelings with your spouse. What where they? Where were you? How did you feel about yourself at the time?

B. When was it most difficult to be open and honest with your spouse? What do you think made it difficult? What sort of mood were you in at the time? What about your spouse? What external influences might have had a bearing on making it difficult?

2. SELF EVALUATION

A. What are the easiest feelings for me to communicate? What are the most difficult? (For these exercises consider such things as praise, joy, sorrow, grief, jealousy, anger, hurt, self-pity, enthusiasm, success, failure.)

B. When I have negative feelings do I lash out, remain quiet, become defensive or withdraw?

3. MISTAKES OFTEN MADE IN COMMUNICATION

A. Thinking I should not be having the reaction or emotion that I am experiencing at the time. "I know I shouldn't feel like this." The fact is, you do. The important thing is to

On Communication

try and discover the cause, not deny the feeling.

B. Believing I show my spouse that I love him by not saying anything about what is bothering me.

C. Not stating clearly what I mean or feel. It is easy to skirt the issue. A person must learn to identify the real significance of an event and state it.

D. Saying nothing for fear of being put down.

E. Failure to speak because I am afraid that my spouse might think less of me for sharing my feelings. I do not want to jeopardize the image I think my spouse has of me.

F. Fear of my partner's reaction. It's risky to tell another how you feel because he may make light of my feelings. I don't want to be vulnerable because it hurts to get hurt.

G. Believing I have to have the last word and always be right.

H. Fear. For a man: the fear of breaking down, crying, feeling silly or weak. For the woman: fear of rejection, criticism, being thought of as a failure.

4. SIGNAL SENDING

Each person sooner or later develops a technique for sending the messages he wants to transmit to his spouse. It is in this area that we most clearly see the truth of the premise that was stated at the beginning of this chapter. We use both verbal and non-verbal methods of communication. In both categories, depending upon our intention, we also send positive or negative signals.

Verbal signals:

    A. The raising and lowering of one's voice. Inflection says a great deal.

    B. Making one's plan or schedule known to your

spouse. Consideration speaks very loudly. Conversely, so does the lack of it.

C. Oral, public embarrassment of one's spouse.

D. Fun chatter — a sign of confidence in a relationship.

Non-verbal signals:

A. Looks (the raising of eyebrows, a questioning look, surprise, turning away).

B. Actions
- Positive: a kiss, a gentle touch, embrace, taking the other's hand, etc.
- Negative: walking ahead of one's spouse, striking, lack of little considerations, etc.

C. Indifference.

D. Silence
- Positive: holding the other in stillness, being there.
- Negative: failure to respond when addressed, sulking, ignoring the other, etc.

Obviously this list of verbal and non-verbal signals does not cover all possibilities, either positive or negative. But if it starts you thinking so you are able to identify what is or isn't taking place in your relationship and if it motivates you to give more careful consideration of the manner in which you can use these methods positively, it will have served its purpose.

5. COMMUNICATING THROUGH COMPLIMENT

There is an interesting little term that is appearing with surprising regularity in literature on personal relationships. It is the term "warm fuzzy." Even though I knew the term was around, I had not been familiar with it.

On Communication

But its meaning was made very clear to me about a month ago — accidentally. An elderly lady in my congregation came to see me about some forthcoming activity. For some reason, and I really don't know if it was her clothes or the happy, pleasant expression on her face, she looked especially nice. I told her so. To my surprise she responded, "Thank you, Pastor, for the warm fuzzy." A "warm fuzzy" is a compliment, an expression of approval or acceptance, or any statement that truly and honestly affirms another person.

In the book, *How To Stay In Love*, Charlie and Martha Shedd have included what they call a "Questionnaire on the Warm Fuzzies." (Copyright, 1980, Charlie and Martha Shedd. Reprinted with permission of Andrews and McMeel. All rights reserved.) It can be an invaluable tool as we use it to evaluate the manner in which we communicate through compliment.

Questionnaire on the Warm Fuzzies

Since "talk, talk, talk" is one of the major secrets to staying in love, the questionnaires in this book are designed to facilitate conversation. Unless otherwise indicated, we suggest that you each answer the questions on your own separate papers. Then if your marriage is ready for it, study each other's answers, compare notes, and set a time for discussion.

1. The last time I paid my mate a compliment was ____
2. The type compliment my mate likes best is ____
3. Five things I especially like about my mate are:

_____
_____
_____
_____
_____

On Communication

4. This list would come as no surprise to my mate, because I verbalize these things and I verbalize them often.
   Yes __
   No __
5. Some things I like about my mate but have never expressed are: _____
6. Words are not the only means of expressing appreciation. I let my mate know I am grateful by specific things such as: _____
7. After thinking through these questions, my performance grade for expression of appreciation is:
   Excellent ____
   Average ____
   Poor _____

6. COMMUNICATING THROUGH INTIMACY

In *Be Good To Each Other*, Lowell and Carol Erdahl state, "To share what is in the depth of mind and heart, to confide our hopes and fears, doubts and dreams is intimacy at its best."

For many people that is extremely difficult to do. It's difficult for several reasons. In some instances it is difficult because a person has never learned how. Words do not come easy for everyone. How often I have heard the statement, "Pastor, I'm not very good at explaining myself but I'm sure you know what I mean."

Then there are some who just plain believe it's not the thing to do. One man expressed his feelings this way. "I just didn't want to burden her. She has enough to worry about as it is." Out of what was obviously a loving motive he was nevertheless denying himself, and her, a real opportunity for growth in understanding.

Others may be too embarrassed to share. To discover one's limitations, the fact that he cannot handle every situation of life, can be painful. Who of us wants our spouse to know our weaknesses? Somehow we need to work at putting aside whatever it is that prevents us from sharing our innermost self with the one we love. You have undoubtedly heard the expression, "Talk is cheap." Serious talk is never cheap. In the first place it might demand that you replace some of your present attitudes with new ones. In the second place it may be priceless since it will open new paths to understanding and compassion for the two of you.

7. COMMUNICATING BY ASKING THE RIGHT QUESTIONS

Earlier in this chapter I spoke briefly about the importance of the *way* in which we ask a question or make a statement. The tone of our voice, the inflection, makes a great difference in what we are attempting to communicate and in the response we get.

Equally as important is the matter of learning to ask the *right* questions. We can close or open communication doors by the questions we ask. Listed below are four good illustrations of the *right* kinds of questions that can be asked as you assess your communication skills.

A. What do you mean?
B. Why do you think you feel that way?
C. What have I done to cause you to feel that way?
D. What can I do to help you feel more at ease with me?

8. COMMUNICATING THROUGH LISTENING

"You tell me you hear me, but you really aren't listening."

On Communication

That is a common complaint made by both husbands and wives. Too often it is true. Jesus recognized the problem when he said, "He who has ears to hear, let him hear" (Matthew 11:15).

Communication is ultimately dependent on another person hearing you or conversely on your hearing him. But to hear, to really hear what another is saying, we have to *learn* to listen. Listening does not just happen. It is a skill that is developed. It is an attitude that is reflected. You know when another person is really listening to you. You know by the responses that are given, both in what is said and what is not said. We do not have to be trained to determine *if* another is listening. But we do have to be trained *to* be good listeners.

Why is listening so important? For several reasons. It's an indication of genuine concern. It's also a sign of acceptance. The intensity with which a person listens also verifies personal worth in the one being listened to. Finally, listening suggests a willingness to learn.

What can a person do to be a better listener?

A. Pay attention. Pay attention to the person and to what is being said. Try to clear your head and to put other matters to the side. The average person speaks at a rate of about 125 words per minute. A person *thinks* at about three times that speed. It is therefore very easy to think ahead of the person speaking. In a sense it is necessary to learn to *think slowly* when you are listening so that you do not mentally jump ahead of the person speaking or allow yourself to be sidetracked by your own thoughts or conclusions.

B. Try not to be defensive. Listen objectively. It is easy for a person to be so sensitive to the possibility of criticism that he hears things that aren't really there at all. Listen to understand and learn what it is that runs deep in your spouse. You are not being attacked. You are being trusted.

C. Ask questions to make sure you are hearing what is really being said. The best way to ask such questions is by restating what you think you heard. "What I am hearing you say is this." (Then state what you heard.) "Did I hear you; did I understand you correctly?" This type of questioning provides a good check on your listening. It also gives the speaker the assurance that you are tracking and hearing what is being said. And it provides opportunity to correct any misunderstandings that might be developing in the conversation.

D. Be responsive rather than reactionary. Reactions tend to breed reactions. Reactions are triggered by emotions. Now there is nothing wrong with emotion. But if in a sharing situation you react emotionally to what is already an emotional moment for your spouse you will most likely discover that the discussion will quickly come to an end. A response that encourages your spouse to continue to explore his or her feelings is much more appropriate.

IN CONCLUSION

One of my teachers once made the following statement. "Listening is loving." Perhaps we could go a step further and suggest that open and honest communication is loving. It is a goal worth working toward, for in the deepest sense it is an intensely personal sharing experience in which each partner sees himself and his spouse as important.

THE "WHY" OF MARRIAGE   **6**

Look carefully then how you walk, not as unwise men but as wise, making the most of the time.
Ephesians 5:15,16

The "Why" Of Marriage

"Why do you want to get married?" The answers to that question are varied. "Because we are in love." "I have found the right one." "I'm tired of living alone."

Beneath those surface answers there is usually a deeper reason. "Because we want to spend the rest of our lives together." That is the *"why"* of marriage. Two people with different backgrounds and different experiences make the decision that they want to spend the rest of their lives together. For better or worse they want to unite in a relationship that remarkably makes the joys, sorrows, disappointments and discoveries of the one the joys, sorrows, disappointments and discoveries of the other.

"Have you not read that he who made them from the beginning made them male and female, and said, 'For this reason a man shall leave his father and his mother and be joined to his wife, and the two shall become one?' So they are no longer two but one" (Matthew 19:4-6).

AND YOU NEED EACH OTHER

We live in a society that is fast becoming a society of numbers. I am identified by credit card numbers, a Social Security number, checking account numbers, computer sort-card numbers, clergy code numbers, and loan numbers only to mention a few. It's getting so bad that when somebody even bothers to address me as, "Hey, you," I feel good about it.

Recently the savings and loan company that holds the mortgage on our house wrote us a letter indicating they would like to use what they call the "direct withdrawal" system for paying our monthly mortgage payment. All we had to do was "sign the enclosed form" upon which our bank would be notified and a computer link would automatically debit the one account and credit the other. We re-

The "Why" Of Marriage

fused to sign it. It is one of the few occasions where we can still force somebody to treat us as persons rather than numbers. If they want to continue to receive our payments they are going to have to put up with our personally signing a check, personally putting it in an envelope, and personally mailing it to them. Perhaps it is only a minor protest but it is still our attempt to keep something of our own personhood. Whether in this type of situation or some other, we all want to assert our individuality.

All of us are faced with the threat of depersonalization today. At the same time we are each faced with the need to be considered as persons. The marriage relationship is one of the few remaining arenas of life in which two people can still enjoy a sense of individuality and personhood and truly support one another in the process.

The uniqueness of your respective personalities attracted you to each other. The qualities and characteristics that moved you to a love relationship need to be encouraged throughout marriage so that you never lose sight of your original intention and decision, "to spend the rest of your lives together."

SOME PEOPLE FORGET

A major part of my post-marriage counseling is now spent with people who have been married from twenty to thirty years. Other counselors have indicated a similar experience. What causes two people to be suddenly seriously troubled about their relationship when they have shared life that long? It is usually the discovery that without realizing it they have grown apart rather than together over the years.

What caused that? Nothing that either of them did deliberately. No two people ever set out to grow apart. Neverthe-

The "Why" Of Marriage

less it happens unless a couple is extremely careful to take the necessary precautions to avoid it.

During the years that a couple is working at raising a family it is terribly easy to become so involved in the lives of the children that they forget why they got married in the first place: to share their lives together. They forget to take time together to nurture their own relationship.

When the children are finally grown and gone the husband and wife suddenly realize that the only thing they had shared in common during these child raising years was the children. In the process they allowed themselves to become strangers to each other.

It's exceedingly difficult to suddenly undo what has been allowed to develop over a period of time. It makes much more sense to do all that you can throughout your married life to make certain your relationship stays strong and fresh.

AN EXAMPLE

One very significant method of nurturing your marriage is to make certain that you regularly have time alone together. That's not always easy — especially after children arrive. But it is extremely important. For it is on those occasions when you are alone together that you will share most intimately, discuss most openly, and remember most vividly the meaningful moments that you have known.

Being away from the children at times is good for them too. In fact, many of the attitudes they will bring into their own marriage later on will be formed by observation. What they see you do, they will do. That which they view as important in your relationship will very likely become important for them as well.

For many years my wife and I have made a point of

The "Why" Of Marriage

spending a part of our vacation time each year away, by ourselves. I happen to be one of those persons who thoroughly enjoys riding a motorcycle. In fact I have either had access to one, or have owned one, since the late forties. I gave Bev her first motorcycle ride in 1950. She wasn't at all sure about it then. But since that time she has become an excellent passenger and enjoys traveling on a motorcycle every bit as much as I do.

Several years ago we were gone on one of our jaunts, having left our three children at home. They were old enough to take good care of themselves.

When we returned from our trip our son Peter reported an interesting conversation he had had during our absence. A member of our congregation had seen him in a local store one evening and was quite surprised by that. The man had assumed that since we were gone our children would be gone too.

The gentleman approached Peter in the store and directed the following comment to him. "What are you doing here? I thought that you would be gone with your folks on vacation." Peter replied, "Oh, they are off somewhere on their motorcycle." To which the man replied, "What kind of an example is that? He talks about 'family' and then leaves the kids at home?" My son's response was one that I shall never forget. I hope the gentleman heard it too. Peter replied, "But my mom and dad need time for themselves too."

That was a very mature response for a young lad. He understood something that undoubtedly will shape his attitude toward his own marriage. Needless to say, I was one proud father. By observation he had discovered an important truth. A relationship has to be nurtured and cared for if it is to grow. In order for that to happen there must be time alone together.

TIME TOGETHER

It is one thing to recognize that two people need time alone together. It is quite another matter to make certain that it happens. In the stress and strain of day to day living partners frequently go their own way even for rest and relaxation.

Listed below are a few general guidelines that a couple can use in arranging time alone together.

1. Time together should be set aside on a regular basis. Every couple can find some period of time (other than going to bed at night) just for themselves. You will undoubtedly have to examine your routines together to determine what the best time alone together is. And certainly the time should be agreeable to both of you. You will be able to find it if you look for it and feel that it is important.

2. Let your time alone together be quality time. The quality of your time may be more significant that the quantity of time. Determine together how you can best spend the time you have. Will it be spent in visiting and sharing? Perhaps your greatest need is to hold each other in stillness and quiet for a while. Or, would you be better served by going for a walk together, engaging in some activity that you both enjoy or in going out for an evening?

3. Experiment in the use of your time together. It is possible to get into a rut even in the manner in which you spend your time alone together. If one of you has a suggestion as to how you would like to spend the time, offer it. Remember that the most important factor is *that* you do it, not *how* you do it.

AND BE FRIENDS

During a recent premarital interview a young lady commented about the relationship she and her fiance had expe-

The "Why" Of Marriage

rienced prior to their engagement. "He was my best friend even before I fell in love with him. And he still is."

It is interesting to note that Jesus used the word "friend" to describe his relationship with his disciples. The word has as one of its meanings, "one attached to another by feelings of deep personal regard" *(The American College Dictionary)*. The manner in which Jesus used the word also implied trust, concern and love.

I suspect that from that perspective most of us have few real friends. We may have many acquaintances whom we label "friends." But there is a difference, isn't there? Real friendship doesn't just happen. It is built and developed through sharing common concerns. It is based on respect of the other and need for the other. Perhaps most importantly, it is grounded in the acceptance of the other as he or she is.

A husband and wife will truly have something extra going for them if they are friends as well as lovers. Friendship means that two people are mutually content to be in one another's company regardless of what they are doing.

That is not to say that a marriage should become such a jealous possessiveness that husband and wife cannot even tolerate friendships outside a marriage. Nor does it mean that two people have to do everything together. After all, even though two people are married they still remain individuals with personal needs for privacy and with certain interests that may differ from those of the spouse.

Yet it does mean that the primary focal point of each partner's effort and attention will be *to* and *in* the relationship so that as much of life as possible can be shared.

In any relationship there are going to be moments when the people involved don't really like each other. That can happen for any number of reasons. But if there is true friendship, then, even on those occasions each will look beyond the moment to see how he can best serve and love the other.

ACCEPTANCE AND FORGIVENESS 7

And be kind to one another, tenderhearted, forgiving one another, as God in Christ forgave you.
Ephesians 5:32

Acceptance And Forgiveness

A pastor friend of mine once commented half jokingly, "If marriages are made in heaven, God has certainly made a lot of mistakes." Looking at the present day divorce rate, for whatever reason they occur, we would probably have to agree with that statement *if* marriages were made in heaven. When two people seem to be particularly well-matched and are getting along good together, the remark is sometimes made, "Those two were meant for each other." Such a comment is very similar in intent to the one made in the opening paragraph. Both, however, convey a dangerous idea about marriage. They are suggesting that God at some point in time takes two people and says, "I will put you and you together, and you and you together," almost against their wills or as though the individuals had no part in the decision making process whatsoever.

While Christians recognize their spouses as special gifts from God, the point we are making is that one's choice of and reaction to his mate are often considered beyond our control. Love and marriage are seen as conditions into which we rather helplessly fall; and, of course, when people fall out of love that, too, is considered beyond their control. This is another widely held modern day myth.

"I CHOOSE YOU"

The fact is, a man or woman has the possibility of a successful marriage with any one of a great number of individuals of the opposite sex. That which makes a marriage to one specific person unique is the fact that there is a decision involved, not merely some vague notion that "this was meant to be." Each person involved makes the decision to commit himself to the other in a more intimate manner than with anyone else. It is as though each said, "Out of all the possibilities, I choose you. I am going to work at our specific relationship. I am going to give myself to you completely and fully in order to make your life rich. I am going to expend my efforts towards you. And believing that God is not only able to, but will, bless this relationship as long as we together live in Christ's love and grow in his love, it will be a successful marriage."

It is when that commitment and awareness are lost that failure follows.

Again, this is not to say that God has no part in the decisions we make regarding a spouse. Certainly a Christian will be sensitive to those attributes and characteristics in another that will build and enhance a relationship. Each will also pray for guidance and direction in making a good decision. The potential for a good spiritual life together should also be given careful consideration.

But there is still a point at which a decision is made. Therefore a person is responsible to a great degree for what actually happens or develops, or for that matter what does not happen or does not develop, in a marriage.

In every marriage there are going to be adjustments that will have to be made by each partner. There will be difficulties and times of tension. There are going to be disagreements and differences of opinion. The outcome of such moments will be determined, however, by the attitudes of the persons involved. And that attitude will be pretty much molded or shaped by one's concern and commitment for or toward the other and the relationship. Once again decision and responsibility are involved. If decision and responsibility rest solidly on a firm faith foundation, then even tense moments can be occasions for growth.

THE GREAT DECISION

A truly meaningful marriage does not just happen. It will

Acceptance And Forgiveness

come only as a result of a decision to die. Does that sound strange? It may at first. But think about this. When I am prepared to put myself aside, when I am willing to sacrifice my own will, my habits, my so-called rights, my dreams and even my ambitions for the sake of another, namely my spouse, the relationship will grow.

Now please do not misunderstand what I am saying. I am not suggesting that you simply turn yourself over to your spouse's whims and wishes thereby giving up on deciding about them yourself by letting someone else decide for you. If your spouse insists on flaunting his or her "I", you accomplish nothing.

Each must die to self so that something *new* can come forth. "The two shall become one" (Matt. 19:5). There is a new life style; there are new goals, shared and common to both; there are new ventures, interests, purposes, and concerns; there are new responsibilities. Most important is the truth that you both have a new purpose, to share life together to its fullest.

THE TWO KEYS

But what makes it all fit together? What is the "key" to a good marriage? After many years of listening to people discuss their relationships, both good and bad, and of working with people who were concerned for their marriage, I have come to the conclusion that there are *two* major keys for a successful marriage: *acceptance* and *forgiveness*.

1. ACCEPTANCE

It's no little word. We all need to feel we are accepted — by someone. Each of us needs to know that it is alright to be who and what we are. There is need for approval. It is important to have a sense of worth. Affirmation, approval

Acceptance And Forgiveness

and a sense of worth all have their roots in acceptance.

It's not news to state that we live in a lonely world. Far too many people have discovered that they can be alone even in a crowd. Lack of acceptance can breed loneliness which in turn can cause depression and despair.

The opposite of acceptance is rejection. Rejection comes easy for most of us. We can reject another because of his age or size. We reject because of differing attitudes or views. The reasons for rejecting another can range all the way from color of skin to bad breath. We do it to each other. And it is done to us. Rejection, rejection, rejection. Most people, sorry to say, experience much more rejection than they do acceptance. Oftentimes the feeling of rejection is called out in words like, "Nobody cares." In a marriage relationship the anguished cry may be, "*You* don't care."

Nevertheless, every one of us needs to feel and be accepted in three different relationships: 1) by God, 2) by ourselves, and 3) by others, specifically our spouse.

There are times when even God seems dead or far away. Faith is weak and trust is nearly gone. In those moments we still have his Word and promise and by the power of the Holy Spirit doubt can be driven back and the presence of God in his love reaffirmed. If in those moments we turn to his Word we can rediscover his love and our acceptance by him. God reassures us of his love with many promises such as, "I have loved you with an everlasting love" (Jeremiah 31:3).

Self-acceptance is also necessary. A few people have an over exaggerated sense of their own importance. But for the most part, for most people, it is the opposite. "I don't like myself. I hate the way I look. I hate the way I feel. I hate my size." And it goes on and on. Very few of us have not felt at some time or another that "I wish I were like. . . ."

Acceptance And Forgiveness

Be that as it may, we undoubtedly need to hear more often than we do that we are each special, very special. We need to be reminded that God has fashioned each one of us and made us unique. Within each of us there are gifts and potentialities. If we place what we are and who we are in God's hands we may be truly surprised by what he can do with and through us. Furthermore, he believed we were worth dying for. That which will free you to most readily accept yourself is the recognition of God's great love for you — just as you are.

Then there is the need to be accepted by others. The most important person in this category is one's spouse. It's not easy to feel that you are always walking on egg shells so to speak. Some relationships are so tenuous that the partners find themselves weighing every word that is spoken or afraid to act lest the other show disapproval.

Acceptance tolerates difference and openness of opinion. Acceptance also indicates understanding. Being understood by another person is a wonderful feeling. Being accepted for who and what you are even when you are not understood is an even better feeling. It may be the closest thing to the love of God that you can ever know from another human being. In like manner it may be the greatest gift you can give to another.

What is greater than to know that we are children of God, engulfed in his love, regardless of what we have said or done? What can be greater than to know we are accepted in love by our spouse regardless of what we have said or done?

There is another interesting spin-out that comes from acceptance. Nothing will encourage another to greater potential quite like acceptance.

Perhaps it is important at this time (and maybe I should

Acceptance And Forgiveness

have said it much earlier) to state that by acceptance I do not mean simply *putting up with the other.* Real acceptance means that you will show your approval when it is due, show appreciation for what is done and shared, build one another up through praise and affirmation, support and encourage in trying times, and assure and reassure by your constant and continuing love.

In an earlier chapter there is an important section on the significance of listening to each other. Listening is truly one of the most valid signs of acceptance since it shows you care enough to really hear what the other is saying.

Perhaps this section can be brought to a conclusion by quoting an old adage. It's one of those statements that has been around for as long as I can remember — and undoubtedly long before that. Nevertheless, it sort of puts this whole matter of acceptance into perspective. *"You can't live on yesterday's love."*

Love needs to be reaffirmed each day, doesn't it? Truly one of the best means you will ever have of affirming your love to your spouse is through your genuine unconditional acceptance of him or her as an authentic, and special, person.

2. FORGIVENESS

Forgiveness is a twin sister to acceptance. Two people who are unable to forgive cannot possibly endure living together as husband and wife.

What was it that freed the prodigal son so that he could truly come home? The acceptance and forgiveness extended by the loving father. It was forgiveness that allowed the son to hold his head high again and not cower under the threat of some future retribution. It was forgiveness that

Acceptance And Forgiveness

lifted the burden and gave him the freedom to function once again as a son.

So it is in the marriage relationship. Conflicts are inevitable. Words hastily and carelessly spoken as a result of conflict will cause hurt. The only real healing for imposed hurt is to ask forgiveness from the one that has been hurt. That's not easy to do. To seek forgiveness implies an admission of guilt. And who of us likes to admit that we are the cause, the guilty one, in any problem? Nevertheless, accepting the responsibility by asking for forgiveness is a true indication of self-giving love.

Not only must we be big enough to *ask*, we must also be big enough to *grant* forgiveness. This may be more difficult than asking since *granting* forgiveness implies forgetting too. To forgive is to forget.

"He keeps bringing it up again and again. I thought I had been forgiven for that a long time ago." Comments like that are not uncommon when two people are experiencing conflict. Have you ever made a statement like that? Has your spouse ever made such a comment about you? If he or she has, you undoubtedly have not forgiven, since you have not forgotten.

If this is so in your life, if it is difficult for you to forget that which caused the hurt (none of us finds it easy to do), admit it to your spouse but then go to your heavenly Father with the problem and ask for his help in the matter.

After all, who understands the need for forgetting any better than God? His forgiveness is unconditional. His forgiving love is also a forgetting love. How we should each rejoice in that. "He remembers our sins no more" (Jeremiah 31:34). Learning from him, as we ask the Holy Spirit to teach us *forgetfulness*, victory will come and we will be free to

Acceptance And Forgiveness

"forget what lies behind and strive forward to what lies ahead" (Philippians 3:13).

Perhaps the best counsel to be found anywhere to conclude this section is from Ephesians 4:31-5:2. "Let all bitterness and wrath and anger and clamor and slander be put away from you, with all malice, and be kind to one another, tenderhearted, forgiving one another, as God in Christ forgave you. Therefore, be imitators of God, as beloved children. And walk in love, as Christ loved us and gave himself up for us, a fragrant offering and sacrifice to God."

COPING WITH JEALOUSY   8

Set me as a seal upon your heart, as a seal upon your arm; for love is strong as death, jealousy is cruel as the grave. Its flashes are flashes of fire, a most vehement flame.

Song of Solomon 8:6

Coping With Jealousy

"The Biblical idea of jealousy includes the range of attitudes from the intense hatred of man for man in envy to the positive emotion of singleminded zeal," states *The Interpreter's Dictionary of the Bible*. From this we see that there are two types of jealousy: jealousy *of*, and jealousy *in behalf of*. The first usage is the one with which most of us can identify. However, like other emotions it is not intrinsically good or bad. It is simply there. When it is turned in upon self it can produce hatred or envy. When it is turned away from self it can produce concern for a good cause and selflessness toward others.

On these pages we will devote our attention to the first type of jealousy. Often referred to as the "green-eyed monster," it can be one of the most destructive emotions within a marriage. A friend of mine suggests that it has its roots in "greed, selfishness and insecurity."

HERE IT COMES

By definition, this kind of jealousy implies a desire for revenge for real or imagined wrongs. Certainly it is not limited to any one age group, or culture or place. It rears its ugly head in every area of man's life.

Children in the same family become arch rivals. A normally loving husband can grow to resent the time his wife spends with their new arrival. A warm, caring relationship between husband and wife can be crippled if one of them shows the slightest indication of affection toward another person. Parents can be emotionally torn by their personal struggle for the undivided attention of their own children. Indeed, nations war against nations as a result of jealousy. No society is free from it. No relationship is immune from its effects.

Even though jealousy has been labeled by some of our

present day so-called liberated people as an outdated emotion, that doesn't make it disappear. When it comes, it still hurts. In fact, it is one of the most all-consuming emotions we experience. It literally seems to take over, doesn't it? One person described it to me as "overwhelming."

THE ROOTS OF JEALOUSY

"Why is a person jealous?" is not an easy question to answer. Sin, of course, is the underlying cause. Yet there are a number of different points of view as to why it crops up in certain individuals and situations.

Some authorities suggest that jealousy has its roots in insecurity. Whenever a person has a poor self-image, a lack of self-esteem, or a feeling of inadequacy he is an ideal target for the jealousy monster.

For example, when I asked one couple what it was that had triggered such an overwhelming feeling of jealousy, the wife responded, "I feel like I never quite measure up. (Husband's name) is always commenting about how well so-and-so does things or how great so-and-so looks. It makes me feel like he really wishes he were married to someone else."

Jealousy also surfaces as a result of a feeling of vulnerability. How would I handle it if I were to lose someone that has become so very important to me? What if another person becomes more appealing to my spouse than I am? How can I know for certain that I am truly meeting his or her needs? How can I compete against those with whom my spouse spends so much time during the working day?

We must not forget possessiveness. How easy to feel that we must have exclusive rights to all of our partner's attention, time and feelings. If, for whatever reason, that doesn't happen it is possible for the "neglected" spouse to feel that there is something seriously wrong with the marriage.

Coping With Jealousy

In dealing with possessiveness it is important to remember that each of us is a many-faceted person with a number of different needs and interests. I am. My wife is. You are. Your spouse is. It is also necessary to realize that no one person can be all things to another. Why? Because of our individuality and our uniqueness. Each of us perceives things differently, understands differently, reacts differently and responds differently.

Therefore, different people will touch you in various ways, according to who you are and according to what or who they are. If we recognize that fact we will also be able to accept the truth that other people may likewise affect our spouse's life as well. And that is not bad. It is natural and normal.

The ultimate question is not *if* we will be touched or affected by other people, but rather what significance do we give to those occasions or allow them to have on us.

Of course it is natural for a partner to be most concerned about relationships that develop, on whatever level, with a member of the opposite sex. That is where the greatest threat to a relationship exists. That is also the point at which jealousy — as a result of one's need to possess — can most easily occur.

I must admit that I don't like the idea that I can't be all things at all times to my wife. But the truth is — I cannot. There are others who will be important to her, fill various needs in her life, and be significant to her in a way I can never be. And that's alright. Because beyond all that there is another ingredient that binds us together: commitment. We said so in our marriage vows. Knowing that commitment is there frees us from the possessiveness that could otherwise choke and smother each other.

Coping With Jealousy

Dependency, for all its virtue, can also be a cause of jealousy. It is not good for two people to be so totally independent that they literally go their own way and do their own thing, whatever that may be, all the time. But it is equally unhealthy if two people become so totally dependent upon each other that all individuality is lost.

Somehow a couple needs to keep the matter of dependency in balance. Even though they are working constantly at building a life together they still need to recognize that each is an individual with distinct creative interests that need to be nurtured.

JEALOUSY IN MEN AND WOMEN

There are some basic differences in the psychological makeup of men and women that often create misunderstandings and provoke jealousy.

Though it is not always helpful to speak in generalities, there are times when generalized statements can assist in clarifying a thought process. Many psychologists and psychiatrists agree that women tend to respond more readily to *intangibles* while men on the other hand respond to *concrete* actions and words. That is to say, jealousy is triggered differently in men and women.

Because of her deep emotional commitment and the feeling that she is literally investing her all in a relationship, a woman may have a greater sense of vulnerability than a man. When her security is threatened, whether by real or imaginary circumstances, jealousy is quick to surface.

Women may find it hard to understand men's actions. Men are often, or at least appear to be, more aggressive and independent. Because of that a man's natural conduct could be understood as a sign of care-less-ness or even unfaithfulness. If a man is quite outgoing in terms of his personality it could be interpreted as dissatisfaction and looking.

Interestingly enough, women seem to be able to cope with jealousy when it has a real cause better than men. Men tend to be totally unreasonable and overbearing if they feel their territory is being invaded.

Imaginary jealousy on the part of either a man or woman is often based on an individual's fears — a feeling of inability to do anything about a situation, powerlessness and one's lack of self-esteem. In either case jealousy will tend to make a person try to fence in the other. In both men and women it has its primary roots in self: self-concern, self-identity, self-interests, self-preservation.

Men and women also tend to express jealousy differently. Women will more often blame themselves through feeling that something is lacking in their own ability to keep a spouse's total interest. A man will feel more put-down or demeaned by his apparent inability to be Mr. Perfect. Ego seems to be a greater concern for men. A man will also tend to blame outside factors and influences in order to compensate for his personal ego deflation.

Men are also more apt to respond in anger. Even though he may not show it as easily or quickly, when it does erupt it may take the form of harsh words and on occasion physical violence. I have had many men personally tell me that they just simply refused to show jealousy. That is to say, they did not want to admit it. But when it did finally come out it came out in an extremely strong way.

Only rarely have I known women to just plain get angry. They are far more likely to carry it all inside. I do recall one instance when a jealous wife verbally tore into her husband and afterward said that she felt much better because of it. Perhaps it did not help their relationship much, but at least it freed her to get it out in the open. I noticed that after the fact she was able to talk about it with much less emotion.

Whatever else may be said about jealousy in men and women, this can be said for certain. Both experience it, both feel it, both suffer the consequences of it. It is painful and often confusing. An individual may try to be as rational as possible about it, but that doesn't stop it. It comes to both at unexpected times — even without deliberate cause on the part of a spouse. It feels bad and both men and women would be hard pressed to believe that anything good ever comes out of it. A lady once expressed her feelings about jealousy like this. "I would be an extremely happy person if I never felt jealous again in my whole life."

NEVERTHELESS

Nevertheless, there is still another question that needs to be asked. Can anything good come out of an experience of jealousy? Of course the answer to that depends upon how a person deals with jealousy.

Essentially it is not so much a matter of coping with jealousy as it is trying to find out what causes it and then dealing with the "why." "Why am I jealous? Why do I feel the way that I do?" If a person honestly sees or senses some lack in himself, it can provide the impetus to do something about it. After all, in any situation the best defense is a good offense. The more sensitive we are to our spouse and our spouse's feelings, needs, and basic make-up, the greater our ability to at least try to respond appropriately. In other words, jealousy can be motivation.

Several years ago a lady expressed deep feelings of jealousy over the conversations her husband occasionally had with other women. He was a college graduate with a Masters Degree. She on the other hand had only a high school diploma. Because of her own insecurity she often would deliberately avoid conversational opportunities by quietly moving into the background. Consequently she felt left out and jealous.

She solved her jealousy problem by pursuing a college degree. Once she accomplished that goal her self-esteem soared. She openly and comfortably entered into conversational relationships much to the delight of her husband. Jealousy was literally a motivation for her to take a course of action that ultimately alleviated the difficulty. One interesting sidelight to this story. He was not even aware of the seriousness of her problem until after her graduation from college. Only then did she finally tell him how she had felt all those years.

He on the other hand had felt he was expressing his love for her by not forcing her into uncomfortable situations. Therefore, when she had elected not to get involved in conversations he honored that as an expression of her personal desires, never realizing the deeper feeling of inadequacy.

HELPS ALONG THE WAY

How does a person cope with jealousy? There is no single, easy answer to that question. But there are a few things you might try as possible helps toward a solution.

First, honestly and openly admit jealous feelings to your mate. They concern your spouse. Oftentimes a partner will discover through conversation that the feelings are totally unfounded. What better way to get rid of them than that? Or, a spouse might help you deal with jealousy by reaffirming your own relationship. It has happened that a wife or husband isn't even aware of the fact that she or he is doing anything that causes jealousy. Open discussion can bring about good preventative maintenance.

Secondly, work on the areas in your life where you feel inadequate so that your own self-esteem can be increased and strengthened.

Thirdly, recognize jealousy for what it is, an emotion, but don't give it more attention than it deserves.

Fourthly, remember always that the Holy Spirit is anxious to impart the fruits that make for wholeness: love, peace, patience, forbearance. So *pray* for them. Far better than anything we can accomplish by our own ability to cope with jealousy is the Spirit's power to quiet a restless and troubled heart.

As a concluding statement let me share with you a quote from Gordon Clanton and Lynn Smith in their book *Jealousy*. "Jealousy is neither proof of love nor evidence of personal failure. It is merely a signal that tells you to attend to your relationship and to yourself."

YOUR MARRIAGE CHECKUP 9

For wisdom is better than jewels, and all that you may desire cannot compare with her.

Proverbs 7:11

Your Marriage Checkup

"One thing I have learned: even if my husband worked late every night and at other times hassled me to the point where I thought I could not stand it a moment longer, I think I should still rather have him come home for a while than not at all. I am so lonesome." So said a lady after having been divorced for nearly two years. Underneath all the hurt that had been generated by years of conflict there still lingered a flickering of love and the remembrance of the good times they had shared. I have no doubt in my mind that she wished, especially now, that the difficulties had been resolved.

It is never easy to live in a tenuous situation. But it may be more difficult to live in the aftermath of divorce even when it looks like it is the only solution possible at the time. As we have stated, God intends for marriage to be a lifelong union. He does not intend for divorce. Consequently, it is never an ideal solution.

AN OUNCE OF PREVENTION

Marriage relationship problems don't happen overnight. They are generated little by little through the accumulation of unresolved problems. They come as a result of failure along the way to recognize, or in some instances admit, the signs that indicate a breakdown in intimacy. "I knew we were in trouble. I just didn't want to admit it." That is the way one man described it.

Whatever the cause, or causes, it is far better to work together toward a solution when trouble is first evident than it is to let things get to the point where reconciliation is virtually impossible.

I am not a person who believes it is healthy always to be "navel gazing" as it is called. That is to say, constantly examining one's self to see how he measures up. It is possible to become so introspective, so inward looking, that there is no time left for living. A person can spend so much time being concerned about *how* he is doing that he never does anything.

On the other hand it is equally dangerous to be totally indifferent to evidences that indicate difficulties are present in a marriage. Somehow there needs to be a healthy balance between these two extremes. The purpose of this chapter is to provide you with some helps you can use to affirm your marriage and spot potential concerns.

1. Affirm your marriage. As you go over the list together you may discover that things are really very good between the two of you. In that case the evaluation helps will compliment you.

2. Point out potential concerns. A word of caution, please. Don't read into an issue more than is really there. In self-evaluation there is always the danger of over exaggerating a situation. Be open and honest with each other but don't make more of a concern than it rightfully deserves.

PRECAUTION

A word of precaution is necessary. If you discover some less than totally satisfactory areas in your marriage, don't automatically assume that your marriage is headed for failure.

Even those that we would label "good" marriages are not without their moments of tension. Any relationship that is built on the imperfect (and we are all imperfect people) is subject to conflict. Therefore, as stated earlier in this book, the concern is never the absence of conflict. It is rather the recognition that it is inevitable but that there are certain steps that can be taken to minimize it. A secret for a

Your Marriage Checkup

successful marriage is early detection and appropriate action as difficulties surface.

Above all, don't get caught in the "let's place the blame on each other" game. Adam and Eve were the first ones to try that method. Then, as ever since, it didn't succeed. Blaming one's spouse accomplishes nothing. I am personally amused by people who play the "blame" game. How ridiculous for a person to carry on in such a manner without remembering that this is the individual he or she carefully selected. It would seem far more appropriate to blame one's self for making such a terrible choice than verbally to annihilate an innocent party. How could the one for whose love at one time you would gladly have died grow to become such a horrible person? It is a question worth asking when you are tempted to start placing blame. Even if you didn't enter marriage in such blind passion, remember the attitudes of love and forgiveness taught in Scripture.

By the way, a book I heartily recommend to a couple that would like to experiment with marriage enrichment exercises in the privacy of their own home is *"Keeping a Good Thing Going,"* by Stephen J. Carter and Charles W. McKinney (published by Concordia Publishing House, Saint Louis, Missouri).

QUESTIONS YOU CAN ASK YOURSELVES

Dr. Roger C. Smith is associate professor of social work at Andrews University, Berrien Springs, Michigan. I asked for his permission to insert his eleven point marital health checkup list in this chapter. He graciously consented to its use. Some of the questions are addressed in earlier chapters. Dr. Smith, however, offers additional insights that can be helpful to you in your discussions.

Your Marriage Checkup

In order to make the experience most meaningful Dr. Smith gives the following suggestions.

1. Choose a relaxed time of the day and week, when neither of you is upset.

2. Invite the Holy Spirit to sharpen your perceptions and soften your reactions.

3. Find a spot where you can sit comfortably, side by side, and share an undisturbed hour.

4. Take turns reading the questions and explanations to each other.

5. Hold hands as one of you reads the questions for the second time. Respond with a squeeze of the hand, or place a check before any question that you feel needs attention in your marriage.

6. Try to focus on what is happening *between* you rather than *to* you.

7. It is healthy to admit shortcomings to your partner in order to inspire hope for change. But you know your mate best and you must decide whether the shocking disclosure of some misbehavior will do more harm than good.

8. After the second reading discuss the questions that reveal need for change in your relationship. Some changes can be brought about by setting priorities on how time and money are spent and planning to set aside some of both for a special purpose. Improvements in habitual attitudes and reactions that hurt your marriage can result from 1) a mutual decision to make specific changes, 2) daily prayer, 3) attention to how the change is progressing, and 4) your mutual readiness to reward even the smallest step in the right direction.

9. If your problems seem too deep-rooted to handle in this way, seek professional help. (One signal would be hos-

Your Marriage Checkup

tilities that make taking the test together impossible.) Your pastor should be approached as readily as legal or medical counselors. Perhaps he will feel that other outside counseling would be helpful and will direct you to someone.

Honest answers to the questions that follow can help you and your spouse detect some of the most common symptoms of an ailing marriage. On the other hand, as suggested earlier, your answers can be very affirming to an essentially good marriage.

Growth never comes without some struggle. This does not necessarily suggest that the greater the struggle the greater the growth. Not at all. Yet it is important to be aware of the truth that a good relationship will take effort — from both partners. Both must be willing to look at themselves honestly and be open to the possibility of change in personal attitudes and actions.

Dr. Smith's checkup list has been printed in such a way that you can check a "Yes" or "No" response. First of all, go through the list together, agreeing on what you believe to be the appropriate response.

After your initial reading and response, go over the questions a second time. *Note that in the paragraphs which follow the checkup there are some suggestions for procedure that should be used during the second reading.* Share these suggestions (and do them) during your second reading and discussion.

Now, to the checkup:

( ) Yes ( ) No 1. Does your spouse regularly receive more "strokes" than "knocks" from you?

( ) Yes ( ) No 2. Is the majority of your pleasant, leisure time shared?

Your Marriage Checkup

( ) Yes ( ) No 3. Do you have at least one three-hour block of togetherness time every two weeks; or at least one getaway weekend every three months?

( ) Yes ( ) No 4. Do you usually settle disagreements with mutual satisfaction and no bitterness?

( ) Yes ( ) No 5. Do you have a satisfying balance of at-home, away-from-home workload?

( ) Yes ( ) No 6. In your relationship is there any game-playing with money, sex, employment, etc.?

( ) Yes ( ) No 7. Is your physical expression of sex mutually satisfying?

( ) Yes ( ) No 8. Is either of you dallying dangerously with someone?

( ) Yes ( ) No 9. Do you feel wanted, loved and appreciated? Even more important, does your mate feel wanted, loved and appreciated?

( ) Yes ( ) No 10. Is anything missing in your relationship that you feel is necessary?

( ) Yes ( ) No 11. Are you still trying your best to have a happy marriage?

HELPS FOR DISCUSSION

1. Does your spouse regularly receive more strokes than knocks from you?

Bare a forearm and demonstrate a "stroke" by a feather-light caress with the finger-tips and a knock with a sharp rap of the knuckles. The stroke represents the afterglow that can be left by positive words. The knock represents the hurt or irritation left by negative words. (Now, tell each other by this method what you think you are getting.)

The spouse who regularly hears more positive than negative statements can take a few negatives now and then. The little attention, the numerous small incidents and simple courtesies of life, make up the sum of life's happiness; and likewise the neglect of kindly, encouraging, affectionate words and of the little courtesies of life helps compose the sum of life's wretchedness.

2. Is the majority of your pleasant, leisure time shared?

Many couples share housework and other necessary activities, and this sharing creates good "feelings." But what about your leisure time? How do you divide it between your spouse and your friends? If your most enjoyable recreation is spent alone or with others outside the marriage, togetherness is losing its appeal.

3. Do you have at least one three-hour block of togetherness time every two weeks, or at least one getaway weekend every three months?

Business can choke out meaningful togetherness, and never-ending rounds of doing things can be an escape from closeness. Togetherness must be planned for. If it occurs on a regular basis, it can provide even more satisfaction to the pair who look forward to it and back on it.

Plan an occasional weekend "away from it all" in a honeymoon atmosphere. Few of us realize how much we are controlled and inhibited by the telephone, the daily schedule, and the constant awareness that the children are nearby.

Christ recognized the connection between relationship and leisure when he counseled his disciples, " 'Come away by yourselves to a lonely place, and rest a while:' for many were coming and going and they had not leisure even to eat" (Mark 6:31).

4. Do you usually settle disagreements with mutual satisfaction and no bitterness?

It would be an unbelievable, long-term miracle if two intelligent individuals who live together never disagreed. Spouses who have serious differences but deny them are merely disguising and postponing trouble. Do you have ground rules for handling differences that allow good feelings for and about each other after the discussion? Some helpful guidelines: 1) The use of physical force is a no-no. 2) No name-calling. Tossing names back and forth does not help either of you. 3) Stick to the subject. Bringing up everything wrong that ever happened confuses the point of contention. 4) No hitting "below the belt." Your intimate knowledge of your spouse exposes his or her vulnerable areas that are unrelated to the problem under discussion. Your anger will tempt you to bring up a shameful or painful shortcoming as a part of your effort to win. Don't.

5. Do you have a satisfying balance of at-home, away-from-home workload?

Are you happy with the way your partner shares work? Does the amount of work you do in the home take into account what your partner does outside the home? A fifty-fifty division of home chores may not be workable or desirable. But even limited participation in household tasks may demonstrate caring and sharing to your partner. The important thing is, not how much you do, but how each of you feels about the division of home chores. How can husband and wife divide the interests of their home life and still keep a loving, firm hold upon each other? They should have united interest in all that concerns their homemaking.

Your Marriage Checkup

6. In your relationship is there any game-playing with money, sex, employment, etc.?

In marriage, sex and money are common topics for arguments. However, the causes of such arguments are usually deeper. "He" controls the money and "she" the sex. (Today's equality between the sexes increases the possibility of reversing who controls what.) Do you use money, sex, or hours on the job to express anger, revenge, a need to control or other disguised feelings?

7. Is your physical expression of sex mutually satisfying?

There is no set frequency for any couple's sexual activity. Are both of you fulfilled and happy with what you do and how often you do it? If not, why not? Have you told each other frankly what you enjoy and what you do not enjoy?

8. Is either of you dallying dangerously with someone?

Many affairs begin innocently enough. One partner will begin to spend a little more time, and to joke with a little more sparkle, with someone of the opposite sex. A common setting for such dalliance is the job. The amount of time spent and the enjoyment of a conversation with a friend tend to increase almost unconsciously and lay a foundation for further involvement. Although such a relationship may seem fun, it must be nipped in the bud by people serious about their marriage.

9. Do you feel wanted, loved and appreciated? Even more important, does your mate feel loved, wanted and appreciated?

In a union of two lives each must minister to the happiness of the other. The need to feel wanted, loved, and appreciated is natural and healthy. If this need is not met (and modern families' isolation from relatives puts a heavy burden on marital partners), the void may be inappropriately filled by over-eating, an ego-boosting affair, or unreasonable demands on the partner.

10. Is anything missing in your relationship that you feel is necessary?

Sometimes one partner feels that something needed is missing from the relationship. He or she may attempt to live with the unmet need by altering expectations or by burying frustrations under all kinds of activities. Either adjustment can mean lessened satisfaction for both. If one needs more affection, and the other is willing to learn to be more affectionate, the needy partner can attempt to reduce his or her need and meet the mate halfway. Reaching out to show affection can be a new and risky experience. If it is a problem in your marriage, are you willing to try?

11. Are you still trying your best to have a happy marriage?

Counselors sometimes find that a couple with long-term marital problems have given up trying to improve the marriage. It is very difficult to change such an attitude — but it is necessary. Both partners must be willing to change.

REMEMBER

Undoubtedly the most important question of all to ask yourselves is this: "What place does Jesus Christ have in our life together?" That is really the bottom line. For it is only as you build your life together on the foundation of worship, a shared devotional life, and the forgiveness of God in Jesus Christ that your relationship will grow to a depth which is beyond human wisdom and ability.

KEEPING THE MAGIC 10

Pleasant words are like a honeycomb, sweetness to the soul and health to the body.

Proverbs 16:24

114

Keeping The Magic

It was not an easy appointment for her to keep. The anxiousness in her voice gave her away. But for some reason she felt compelled to explain her decision to me.

"Pastor, Ted and I are getting a divorce." I was more disappointed than surprised. In spite of their enthusiasm for getting married there was something about their attitude and behavior that gave me an uncomfortable feeling right from the start. I just couldn't pinpoint it.

Our premarital sessions together had not raised any significant questions. In fact, after several weeks of meeting together and working through some mutual concerns, I came to the conclusion that the two of them could make it if they really worked at it. For my part that conclusion had represented a dramatic change in view, because early in our sessions I had encouraged them to wait a while until they knew each other a little better. I had even gone as far as to suggest that they consider breaking off the relationship for a time. But in the inimitable fashion of young people's persuasiveness, they had managed to convince me that everything was fine and that they wanted very much to be married. They were both "so much in love."

She came to my office less then six months after their marriage. Their relationship had degenerated to the point of constant quarreling and bickering. They apparently shared nothing in common, not even the desire to stay married.

The young woman summed up her feelings with the following statement. "Pastor, I am afraid that we were more in love with the *idea* of marriage than with each other." In retrospect, I will have to agree with her. I wish I had been smart enough to see that clearly prior to their marriage. But as anyone who is involved with marrying people knows, that's not always easy to do. At least it isn't for me.

Keeping The Magic

So people continue to get married: some for the right reasons and some for the wrong reasons. Even though I cannot always make a correct judgment prior to a marriage on whether or not two people are really suited for each other and will be able to make a go of it, I have come to the conclusion that there are several very important factors involved after marriage that are necessary to keep it going and growing. But before I address the positives that will assist you in keeping the magic in your marriage, let's look briefly at two categories of negatives for which you should be on the alert.

LURKING WOLVES

Have you ever confronted a wolf face to face? A wolf is a "large wild carnivore that is swift-footed, crafty, rapacious, and destructive." I hope you never do meet a real, live wolf other than in a zoo.

There are wolf-type situations that can destroy or even devour a marriage if a couple is not observant. The first of the two that we will discuss is:

1. BOREDOM

A. Boredom with self. "Nothing new or exciting ever happens to me." That is a common statement offered by both husbands and wives. "My life is in a rut." "I'm not going anywhere." "I'm expected always to be the same: lovable, accessible, available."

B. Boredom with job. "Well, tomorrow is Monday again. Back to the same old routine. Fight the paper work. Fight the boss. Fight the regulations." "Sometimes I don't think I can stand it one more day." "I don't enjoy what I am doing but I don't know what else I could do." "All it gives me is a paycheck."

Keeping The Magic

C. Boredom with family. "Tuesday it's music lessons. Wednesday it's church. Thursday it's this. Friday it's that. It's the same old thing, over and over again."

D. Boredom with one's mate. "We never do anything exciting together anymore." "All he wants to do is sit at home in front of the television." "She used to try and look pretty once in a while." "He's gotten to be a work-aholic. I never see him." "We never sit and talk like we used to."

The fact is, life can be monotonous at times. We all experience the dullness that comes from being caught up in routines. Far too often one day seems to be just like the next. Sameness is not always blessedness. When there is too much of it our heads and hearts can yearn for something new; a new adventure, a new relationship, a new experience. Anything to change the routine. Anything to alter the sameness.

The question we each have to ask, specifically with regard to marriage is, "What am I personally doing to make our marriage more exciting?" It's very easy to lay the blame for "boredom" on the other party without realizing that we might be the major contributing factor because of our own care-less attitude.

By my actions I might inadvertently give my spouse the idea that things are just the way I like them, thereby suggesting that if she really loves me she will leave things as they are while all the time I am inwardly looking for a different response from her. How can she be blamed for not knowing, especially when I do nothing to suggest either a need for or a desire for change?

2. LIVING WITH FALSE ASSUMPTIONS

A. Waiting for tomorrow. "Things would be so much better if I only had a different job." "What we need is a new house." "When I get my raise it will be easier."

B. Things will get better with time. "After the kids are gone, *then* we will have time for ourselves." "Once we get the mortgage paid we will have a few extra dollars to do things." "When we get a little older we won't have quite as much responsibility."

C. Time heals all wounds. "If I don't say anything about it, perhaps it will go away." "I'll just be quiet and not make a big deal of it." "I don't want to cause an upset or make waves." "Things aren't all that bad."

D. Looking toward retirement. "Then we will have the freedom to do what we want." "Once I have saved enough for retirement we can go places."

Whenever a relationship is built on a false assumption it is inevitably destined for failure. Essentially all four of the previously listed assumptions (and this is not a complete list by any means) state the same thing. Given a different set of circumstances things would be different.

What is important to remember is that *things are as they are now*. A relationship is not just a future event. It either *is* or *isn't* now. Therefore, the joy that you experience in your marriage is not dependent on tomorrow but rather on what you *together* do with and make of your todays.

ALONG THE WAY

The world is filled with "How To" books. It doesn't need another one. Most of them make me feel like a failure anyway. They all talk about how to succeed, how to be important, how to become rich, how to this and how to that. Furthermore, on those occasions when I have earnestly tried to follow the directions, I have been disappointed because it never seems to work for me.

Keeping The Magic

Such an experience makes me reluctant to suggest that you do or try certain things in order to keep the magic in your marriage. If you will, however, accept the following statements not as "how to's," but as suggestions that could make a difference in your relationship, they may be helpful. They are offered in that context.

1. Treat and respect each other as persons. Neither of you is intended to be a slave of the other. Each is an individual with personality, character, abilities, needs, goals, desires and possibilities. Encourage each other. Support one another in times of need. Never under any circumstances treat your spouse purely as a means of satisfying your sexual needs and desires.

2. Pay attention to little things. This is a two-sided coin. One side asks you to give attention to the little things. Little things are important. Performed in love at the right time, little courtesies can send a large message. Birthday and anniversary remembrances are significant moments in your spouse's history. Be sensitive to the little things that you know offend or hurt your mate.

On the other side of the coin you are asked to acknowledge all those meaningful little things that your spouse does for you. When was the last time you thanked the other for performing a menial task that is so easily taken for granted? A friend of mine whose wife has become ill with cancer made the following comment. "I never really realized all the little things she did until I had to start doing them myself."

3. Remember that happiness is dependent on giving, not getting. You belong to each other — not to yourself. Let your life be totally consumed by doing all you can to make your spouse's life rich and full. The greatest joy you can ever experience is that which comes from seeing joy in the life of

Keeping The Magic

another to whom you have given a gift, especially if it is the gift of yourself.

It will probably surprise your spouse, too. Several weeks ago on a Saturday morning, for no real reason other than I thought it would be a nice thing to do, I prepared breakfast for my wife and served it to her while she was still in bed. She almost fell out from shock.

Because she is a gracious lady she did not ask "What are you up to," or "What do you want," or "What's the occasion?" She accepted it and enjoyed it. It was a good moment for her — and for me — since in a small way I had reaffirmed the joy that comes from giving at an unexpected time.

4. Say "I need you" to each other. The people in my congregation to whom I am most likely to respond are those who tell me that they need me. That gives me a sense of worth and importance. When I am needed I have value. My self-esteem will rise at least ten points.

An individual who is always able to handle things by himself is not much fun to be around. A mate that has no need of you because of his or her own capabilities to do everything well and always be on top of things emotionally makes you feel about as important as a breath of air in a windstorm.

How often I have heard a partner in a marriage literally cry out with the words, "He doesn't need me." "She seems to get along just fine without me." Everyone of us needs to be needed. That is especially true in the closest and most personal relationship any of us will ever have: marriage.

Let your mate know that you need him or her for more than an occasional romp in bed. If you can only learn to say so you may be surprised by the openness your spouse suddenly has towards you.

Keeping The Magic

We can shut people out of our lives or we can let them in. Saying "I need you" opens doors through which people are happy to walk. Your spouse is no exception.

5. Learn to touch. Not only with words but with your hands. Touching and being touched is marvelously personal and sensual. Take the time to touch each other physically. There is a place for fondling, caressing and embracing in marriage. And it is not essential that your touching always result in intercourse. Indeed you may discover that you prefer not to have intercourse on occasion. Why? Because intercourse involves performance. Touching without feeling that it must end in intercourse can free you to enjoy the experience for its own value.

6. Give each other a little room to function as individuals. Many today refer to this as "space." "I need some space for myself," a spouse will say. What is really being said is that there is a desire for a little freedom.

Relationships can be so overpowering, so demanding, that a person can actually feel smothered with love. There needs to be a balance between one's desire for the undivided attention of his spouse and the recognition of a mate's need for some freedom. After all, love in the truest sense is freeing, not possessive. It frees a person to be who and what he is, to develop his own interests, and to respond out of desire, not ownership.

7. Finally, build your relationship on the foundation of Jesus Christ. This counsel can never be stated too often.

It is only when a person is filled with the love of Christ that he will have love to give. You cannot give what you do not possess. Only as individuals experience the forgiveness of God in Christ will they be able to be forgiving. Only after one has known mercy will he be merciful. Only as a person understands his own acceptance by God through grace will he be able, without qualification or stipulation, to accept another.

As the Holy Spirit leads us to understand who and what we are in our relationship to God through the redemptive work of Jesus Christ, we will be enabled to live a life that will fulfill the one with whom we have been united.

Christ's example is our one and only model. "But whoever would be great among you must be your servant, and whoever would be first among you must be your slave, even as the Son of man came not to be served but to serve, and to give his life as a ransom for many" (Matthew 20:26-28).

God bless you in the joy and struggle of building your special life together.